Life's Golden Nuggets

Lessons to Live By

Guy Bouchard
and
Jenna Sartor

WESTBOW
PRESS®
A DIVISION OF THOMAS NELSON
& ZONDERVAN

Scripture taken from the Holy Bible, NEW INTERNATIONAL VERSION®. Copyright © 1973, 1978, 1984, 2011 by Biblica, Inc. All rights reserved worldwide. Used by permission. NEW INTERNATIONAL VERSION® and NIV® are registered trademarks of Biblica, Inc. Use of either trademark for the offering of goods or services requires the prior written consent of Biblica US, Inc.

This book is a work of non-fiction. Unless otherwise noted, the author and the publisher make no explicit guarantees as to the accuracy of the information contained in this book and in some cases, names of people and places have been altered to protect their privacy.

WestBow Press books may be ordered through booksellers or by contacting:

WestBow Press
A Division of Thomas Nelson & Zondervan
1663 Liberty Drive
Bloomington, IN 47403
www.westbowpress.com
1 (866) 928-1240

Because of the dynamic nature of the Internet, any web addresses or links contained in this book may have changed since publication and may no longer be valid. The views expressed in this work are solely those of the author and do not necessarily reflect the views of the publisher, and the publisher hereby disclaims any responsibility for them.

Any people depicted in stock imagery provided by Thinkstock are models, and such images are being used for illustrative purposes only. Certain stock imagery © Thinkstock.

ISBN: 978-1-5127-5565-7 (sc)
ISBN: 978-1-5127-5564-0 (e)

Library of Congress Control Number: 2016914456

Print information available on the last page.

WestBow Press rev. date: 10/4/2016

Dedication

To my amazing, dynamic wife, Robyn, thank you for supporting and pushing me to be my best throughout our marriage. Thank you for slowing me down when I go too fast and speeding me up when I go too slowly. God gave me the perfect woman to enjoy life with. I wouldn't be half the man I am today without you.

To my incredible children who are having a profound impact on the world by working to make it a better place. You were my inspiration for creating this book. My hope is to bless, encourage, and inspire you, your generation, and those that follow. This is for you.

To the team at Global, thank you for your hard work, energy, and dedication. Your efforts are truly helping to improve the world. Without your diligence, I would not have had the time and energy to write this book. Thanks for everything you do.

Contents

Foreword

I have to tell you where the title *Life's Golden Nuggets* came from. My mother was an amazing lady and my biggest supporter growing up. She taught me early in life that if you read a self-improvement book that offers one or two nuggets of wisdom to apply to your life, it is worth the time and effort. I once heard a quotation from an astronaut: "If you miss the moon by one degree, you will be thousands of miles off course."

The idea of these nuggets is to help you correct or refine your course in hopes that you can achieve your life's goals and purposes. There will be nuggets you may be at ease with and some that may feel uncomfortable, requiring work. Either way, I challenge you: if the shoe fits, wear it.

I wanted this book to be friendly to all audiences and to serve as a subtle draw to the Christian life. But as we started compiling chapters, it was apparent that my Christian beliefs permeated all my stories and life lessons. Adding Jenna's voice, the book became even more God centered. I believe, even if you are not a Christian, the Bible is the ultimate guide to living a happy, successful life.

When reading these nuggets, please don't think that we are assuming a self-righteous attitude or claiming to be masters of every area covered or idea presented. Sometimes we can recognize a truth even if we haven't mastered it. Our primary goal in writing this book is to help people live more joyful and fulfilling lives. If one of these nuggets helps readers avoid a land mine or seize a fortunate opportunity, then we have succeeded.

Introduction

Life is full of twists and turns, up and downs, good and bad. Few things stay the same. Many things fade away, and a lot of things abandon us. How do you know where to invest your life? How do you figure out what is important? How do you handle the hard times in a way that keeps you moving forward? How do you learn to laugh at yourself when you fail? Are you determined to enjoy the journey no matter how many times you have to get back up and begin again?

There are many ways to learn these things. Many avenues can lead to finding meaning or purpose in all that life throws your way. Opportunities arise for learning when to move and when to stand still. A plethora of voices offer advice on when to speak and when to stay quiet. Our world is bursting with information—much of it good—to help you and me live enjoyable lives we are proud of.

This book is one of those tools. It isn't written as a final authority on any one topic. Simply put, it is a collection of insights on everyday encounters that everyone on earth faces. This book provides navigation tools for finding joy while becoming who we were created to be. It is nothing more than one man sharing his journey of discovery and lessons learned to anyone willing to receive them.

We have sectioned this book out in nugget portions so that you can enjoy bite-sized encouragement for whatever is happening in your life. Within each chapter are action steps or questions to ponder. Whatever you put into these steps and questions you will get out of them. If you want to read straight through (as you might any ordinary book), then go for it. However, if you need specific guidance for a particular area of life, feel free to check the contents page and flip right to that section.

Lastly, we want to encourage you to laugh, smile, and enjoy the journey of your life. This book contains content that's meant to encourage a personal response and maybe some motivation for change. Enjoy the work of finding a better state of mind. Experience your growth as fun exploration. For example, it's awesome to make people laugh. Sometimes people laugh with us, and sometimes people laugh at us; either can be beneficial. Laughter is music to the soul. Sometimes you have to fight for your joy, but it's worth the battle. You are worth fighting for.

So dive in, and if you take away even just one nugget that can increase your experience of living a fuller life and enjoying this awesome journey, then our work is a success. We are all in this together, we all need each other, and we are all better together!

Thanks!
Jenna Sartor
Certified Life Coach and coauthor of *Life's Golden Nuggets*

Chapter 1

Winning Starts in Your Thoughts
Choosing What You Think Upon

I have yet to run into a highly motivated and successful individual who spends much time thinking about how many problems he or she has. Across the board, I have found that successful, happy people think high thoughts. They spend their time clarifying the vision of what they are building; when they run into a problem, their thoughts are geared toward finding solutions.

You are a winner. You are a one-of-a-kind solution bringer to the world around you. You have a unique influence on the earth that no one else possesses. The answers are within you already. Becoming you is the greatest gift you can give to the world. The first step to becoming you is to decide to think only the thoughts that will get you there.

Nothing I enjoy in life is fully because of me. It is God who has allowed me to enjoy a relationship with Him, a happy marriage, a healthy family, wonderful friends, vibrant church communities, success in business, and so much more. Together with God, I have been incredibly blessed. Yet, I fully understand now that I'm just one disaster away from my demise. Every day, every experience, and every life that touches mine are truly gifts. Once I received this revelation, I was humbled. I made a decision to become intentional about thanksgiving.

When you choose to give thanks for all that is right in your life, an overpowering force disables your problem-oriented mentality. When you gain the perspective of how big God is and how much He has done through, in, and for you daily, you really begin to see how small every situation is in comparison to Him.

The next step to consider is what you are allowing to occupy your mind. I love the phrase "Garbage in, garbage out." For

> Choose to give thanks for all that is right.

example, do you read books that help you grow (hopefully this is one!), or do you read trash? Maybe you don't read much at all. Do you watch too much TV or play videogames in your free time? Trust me, success will not fall in your lap, so spending all your time doing things that are not moving you toward your goal or vision is a sure way to stay stuck.

I believe this principle can also apply to music, movies, and friends. I'm not implying that it is necessary to exercise or read the Bible every free moment you have. I love classic rock, and the message isn't always positive, but my goal is to balance my nonproductive activities with activities that challenge me to stretch, grow, and overcome.

I also have to be aware of the people I'm surrounding myself with. Do they agree with the message about where my life is going, or do they prefer me where I used to be?

It is imperative that those around you—the individuals whose voices may influence your decisions—have a renewed, up-to-date vision of your purpose and mission in life. They are the ones who can help you keep going when you want to give up, or they can help you remember the call when you get knocked down and forget. Your mind is powerful, and victory truly starts there, but you will not be able to achieve your purpose alone.

Some days, you will get hit hard. Life can be painful and depressing. It is true for all of us. The difference lies in how we respond to life's difficulties. You get to decide who you are going to be, and then be that person no matter what comes your way. In other words, before the storm hits, you need to have a plan of how to overcome it. Before it gets too hard, have your strategy prepared. Consider how you will navigate through and keep moving forward throughout the stormy time. A strategy is what overcomers employ, and you are an overcomer if Jesus lives in you.

Mindset Goals

1. How much time will I spend each day taking in quality material to help me grow?
2. Who in my life encourages me? Speaks life into me? Believes in who I am more than I believe in myself?
3. How can I invest in strengthening those relationships?

4. When I want to spend my time engaging in nonproductive activities such as music, video games, or television shows, how am I going to balance that choice with positive, productive activities?

5. What productive activities can I do to encourage growth, strength, stretching, and overcoming?

6. How can I choose ahead of time, before it gets too hard, to fix my mind on what is true, good, right, or noble?

Chapter 2

Victor or Victim?

The Power of Overcoming

I was in bed recently with my breathing machine for sleep apnea—with an aching back and suffering with heartburn from a piece of pizza I ate too late—and I thought, *I'm falling apart!* Immediately, I combated that thought with, *I'm so blessed.* I had an opportunity to enter into self-pity in that moment, but I chose not to. I chose to fix my mind on what was good. Even though the pain was real, it was not what I wanted as my focus.

To walk in a life of victory, there is really no room for being a victim. You have to choose what to think about and what type of experience you want to have. Good and bad circumstances are happening to everyone all the time. The difference between victims and victors is how you choose to respond to circumstances.

At the root of every victim mentality that wants to rule our lives is a sense of entitlement. When I say entitlement, I am referring to a sense of deserving to have or enjoy things you haven't earned yet.

We all see the lives of people on television who are promiscuous, wealthy, and have all the toys. These fantasy lives seem harmless enough, and they all allude to happiness. But this leads us to believe that we need all of those material possessions to be happy. And yet, it mostly isn't within our reach. When we compare our lives to the

> In victory there is no room for being a victim.

subconscious messages we are bombarded with, we can easily find ourselves dissatisfied with reality. How do we combat this?

I have found a few really important keys that help me live intentionally and victoriously. The first one is to be thankful on purpose. When I begin to feel the weight of what is really wrong building up, I make a conscious choice to give thanks to God for everything He has freely given me, including all the blessings I have been able to fully experience and enjoy.

The second key is to train your brain to flag negative thoughts. You cannot allow yourself to think just any thoughts you want to think. You have to decide who you want to be and where you want to end up, and then think only the thoughts that will aid you in getting there, disregarding any contrary messages.

The second key directly leads into the third, which is to have a personal mission or purpose. If you miss this key, you risk missing the whole point of your life.

I have found that once I got clear on the mission for my life, all the battles along the way were not as huge as they once seemed. If you do not know why you are living your life or why you are engaging in or serving a particular mission, even a small bump in the road will seem like a mountain that is too hard to climb. Yet, when your heart beats with passion for a particular purpose, nothing will be able to stop you. You will begin to understand that every force trying to impede you isn't really after you but the mission you are advocating for. It's bigger than you. When you get hit, you will simply, as General George Patton put it, "improvise, adapt, and overcome." This will continually help you to become a better version of you.

Do these thoughts leave you wondering how to get clear on your purpose? Here are a few soul-searching questions to help you gain that revelation.

1. What moves you to tears?
2. What injustices make you feel angry?
3. What makes you experience happiness?
4. What are you naturally good at?
5. What are you afraid of not happening in the world?
6. What group of people do you want to reach?
7. If you could teach anything, what would you teach?
8. At the end of your life, what do you dream of being remembered for doing, changing, becoming, or creating?

We have been created uniquely with a specific plan and purpose. Once we get clear on it, the world will be ours to change for the good!

You may have been a victim in your lifetime, as most of us have, but you can still choose to have the mentality of a victor and receive an upgrade in your life's experience. The choice is truly yours!

Chapter 3

Who Are You Going to Please?
Getting Your Priorities Straight

Have you ever found yourself in a situation where someone will be unhappy no matter what choice you make? What do you do? How do you decide whom you will please and whom you will seemingly let down?

In my early years, this issue was a constant struggle for me. I would try to do everything to make everyone happy—and it was always a complete failure. The pain I felt and the pain I caused others was nearly lethal—especially in my marriage. I dealt my wife numerous wounds by not intentionally deciding who to please.

I learned quickly that if I was saying no to something, I was inversely saying yes to something else. Once I realized I had to make a decision, I wasn't sure how. I knew this uncertainty was hurting my life and causing me to hurt others.

Then I asked God to help me. He faithfully gave me the revelation I needed to experience freedom in this aspect of life. I realized, first and foremost, that I was called to please God. He sacrificially loved me and completely accepted me so that I might live out the plans for which He created me. Once I really began to receive all that He did for me—far more than I deserved—my natural response to such love was my desire to please Him.

Next, I chose to please my wife. My beautiful wife is incredibly gracious to me and deserves far more than I can give her. Our love for each other has turned my heart toward wanting to please her even when I do not agree with her. And then, it is my heart's desire to please my children. I love them deeply, and my truest desire is to do all that I can to support, encourage, and lead them into what God has purposed for them.

Initially, making this transition was painful. But now that my priority list is clear and narrowed down, my decisions have been far less stressful. I discovered that a lack of priorities was the cause of much worry; this lack stole my peace and provided no further resolution. What was once a huge stressor in my life is now virtually nonexistent. What a testimony of how powerful asking and receiving a revelation from God in a problem area of life can be!

What steps can you take if you are facing a similar dilemma?

1. Realize that you cannot make everyone happy.
2. Ask God to show you the narrow list of people whom you are to please.
3. Once you make that decision, stick with it, and invite peace to enter into it.
4. Give yourself permission to say no, and enjoy what that allows you to say yes to.

9

Chapter 4

Strengths and Weaknesses

Embracing Who You Are

We all have strengths and weaknesses in every area of our lives. Having strength is nothing to boast about, and feeling weak is nothing to be ashamed of. These aspects of our lives cause us to need others, to be interdependent in relationships, and to help us value and appreciate each other.

One of the reasons I really enjoy my life right now is because I am able to work using only my strengths, and that is really fun. It is enjoyable to focus on and do what I am naturally gifted to do. However, it hasn't always been this way. When Global (our company) was small, I was everything from the IT guy to the plumber and all job titles in between. Little by little, as the business grew, I began to exit out of my weaknesses by replacing myself with someone who was truly gifted and needed in various areas. As I have been able to pursue this strategy, the business has flourished and runs like a well-oiled machine with or without me.

Early on, I realized I needed to be intentional about surrounding myself with people who complimented my strengths. Most of us, however, tend to surround ourselves with people who are like us. It is more comfortable and yet exponentially less beneficial.

In the beginning years of our company, we had a manager with many of the same strengths Robyn and I had. We would have fantastic, exciting meetings that birthed amazing ideas. And then nothing happened. We were all idea people. As we recognized this disconnect, we made a transition and hired a manager who was gifted in analytical strategies and could create systems to carry an idea into action. As a result of this adjustment—the intentional joining together with someone with polar opposite gifts—the growth of our company has been tremendous.

Do you see how the plain fact of nothing happening was an indicator that something was wrong? If something is healthy, it bears fruit.

If you have been wondering how to identify your strengths, take a moment to step back, look at your own life, and ask yourself some powerful questions.

1. What am I doing that is working?
2. What are my natural gifts? What do I do well that brings joy to others and to me?
3. What do I have that adds value to other lives, companies, or visions?

Strengths are an indicator, an arrow if you will, of the reasons you are placed on earth. God uniquely created you and gifted you with specific purposes. I want to challenge you to be aware of your weaknesses but not focus on them. Spend more energy becoming aware of your strengths, and choose to continue developing them. Also, as you become aware of your weaknesses, be on the lookout for others who have strength where you are weak. For instance, if you aren't great with money, find someone who is, and add value to them with your strengths.

There is another way to become aware of your strengths and weaknesses. This one takes a little more courage and will equip you with more confidence to live into your strengths. You can

> If something is healthy it bears fruit.

ask the people in your life—whom you trust and respect—their evaluation of who you are with regard to certain aspects of life. For instance, when I want someone to evaluate the spiritual aspects of my life, I will probably consult my pastor or spiritual mentor. They would not be the same people I would ask about my strengths in business. Some of the greatest gifts of my life are the people who lovingly, consistently, and honestly discuss who I am and how I am or am not gifted.

A cautionary word: one last aspect of this journey is about being offended. When you open yourself up to others and ask them about your strengths, they may not give you the answers you expect to hear or even ones you want to hear. So I urge you to consider how expensive being offended could be. For example, one of my weaknesses is that I am terrible on video. I would try to shoot videos for my company, and the effort was always forced and awkward. My team finally shared how terrible I was; as I received this as truth, it was really a relief. I could have become offended and allowed it to be a point of contention with my team.

I could have continued trying to do something I wasn't meant to do. But truly, when I desperately try to be good at something outside my gifting, the result is burdensome. Even though I was willing to keep trying and working at the videos, it was actually a relief when I released that responsibility.

Working into your strengths will be a great joy and gift for those around you. I know a woman who is an accountant, and she recalls that even as a little girl she played at being an accountant. It is her heartbeat, passion, and strength. If I worked for her, I would be fired. I would transpose numbers and mess everything up. I was not created to be an accountant, and that is okay.

When you watch someone who is a deeply gifted actor or musician, you receive such a beautiful blessing by watching that person display his or her strengths. I believe everyone's strengths are a gift to others.

Thoughts to Ponder

1. Who can I ask about strengths that they recognize in my life?
2. Am I willing to make small shifts to begin working into my strengths?
3. Do I currently need to be relieved of a weakness I am endlessly trying to strengthen? Is this effort stealing my joy and causing me frustration?
4. Am I willing to surround myself with others who are different than me?
5. What did you dream about being when you were a kid?

Chapter 5

On Road Rage

Overcoming Anger

I have to drive somewhere each and every day. That is something you and I most likely have in common. Most days, I am presented with opportunities while driving to get angry, say hurtful things toward others, and have my blood pressure rise. However, I have made a small change recently, which is really upgrading my experience on the road and is positioning me to have better days.

When someone drives in a manner that gets under my skin, I have decided ahead of time to pray for that person instead of getting angry or raging about them. (Go with me here for a second before deciding that it seems silly or not worth reading.)

You never know what people are going through. You do not know why they are in a hurry. As a matter of fact, you know nothing about them, let alone why they are being aggressive drivers.

It is not wise to judge people by your brief interaction with them. Mostly, it is unproductive to judge people at all. On the contrary, it is always productive to pray for others. It helps me and it helps them. I cannot seem to maintain my intense, negative emotions toward others when I am praying for them. I pray for them to be blessed and have their needs met. If they do not yet know our Savior, I pray they will soon have that opportunity and give their lives to Him. This is only one among several prayers that strike my heart for other individuals.

> You never know what people are going through.

This practice has saved me from potential road rage incidents. Now, whenever I am interacting with others and I become aware of my natural bent toward stress, anger, or fear, I make the decision to pray instead of react. It's a small shift that has completely changed my experience of life.

The challenge is to look objectively at ourselves and get real about what triggers our rage, fear, offense, anger, or any other defensive reaction. Then, we decide ahead of time to pray instead of reverting to our destructive reactions. Not only will our experiences in life be far more enjoyable, but those around us will also get to enjoy us more.

Here are a few questions you can ask yourself to gain some awareness about what triggers your negative reactions.

1. When was the last time you felt rage (on the road or otherwise)?
2. When was the last time you overreacted to a situation? (We all have, so don't buy into any shame attached to it.)
3. What are you afraid of?

4. How do you act when you feel intimidated?
5. How do you respond when something unexpected happens in your day?
6. Have you ever had a bad moment by which you would hope not to be judged?

That's just a start. Becoming aware of your own emotional reactions will help you begin to exercise self-control and enjoy your one chance at life. Make a small shift and expect *big* change!

Chapter 6

Fighting Fair

Controlling Your Emotions

Early on in life, I actually enjoyed getting involved in a good fight. I always thought my way was right, and I wouldn't back down. I was born to fight for what I really believe in. The change that has occurred over time, however, isn't just how I engage in battle but what I fight for.

When you find yourself exchanging explosive words with someone you love, it becomes important to identify motive. Why am I fighting this fight? What do I want to get out of it? What am I willing to risk losing to achieve my goal? Is it worth it?

How often can you take the time to process through your motives in the heat of battle? For me, it was next to never. It was afterward, going through the debris left over from the verbal punches, when I would realize the damage done—how much was lost and how little was gained. In an effort to be right, I would destroy the most precious treasure—the other person.

Why do I say a person is the most precious treasure? I say it because through the teachings of Jesus, I've learned that the two most important actions in life are to love God and love others. This knowledge alone shows me how deeply important people are to Him. If I truly love God, then I will love those He loves; by doing so, I obey His commandments.

Once I chose to gain God's perspective on the people in my life, protecting our connection became my chief objective. I no longer wanted to fight over being right.

And how do you intentionally protect connection?

You listen.

One key to listening well is to consider, before the conversation begins, that you may be wrong. The other person may be right. It is okay to not be right all the time. In fact, some of the wisest people I know have the courage to admit when they are wrong. When you listen with intentionality and a humble spirit, you will be amazed by how much more you hear. A great way to let someone know you are listening is to repeat back to them what they just shared with you. Oftentimes, situations can be resolved by simply hearing each other correctly.

> The most precious treasure- the other person.

You open your heart.

Remember that you value the person over winning a fight, being heard, and being right. Opening your heart means positioning yourself to love others well. Opening your heart by allowing yourself to be real, known, and vulnerable creates a safe space for the person you are talking with to be open in return. This kind of vulnerability gives permission for the conversation to reach the root of the issue—not just bandage over the symptom that brought it to the surface.

You communicate clearly.

Words such as *always* and *never* usually aren't true when it comes to grievances. Try your best to eliminate these words from your vocabulary. Be mindful of pointing a finger and blaming. Choose instead to own what you are feeling and explain why. Give the other person as much time as he or she needs to share heartfelt matters; don't rush or speak over him or her. Such patience will go a long way toward creating a safe environment where a solution can be reached.

Reach a solution together.

No one likes to keep shooting if the other person ceases fire. This is one sure way to help an argument simmer down. Once the heated emotions have cooled off, a door opens to share what is truly painful or to identify the actual place of disconnection in your relationship. Once you really listen to each other, there is an opportunity to reach a solution to the problem. This in turn opens a deeper connection. It's a win for both because the result is love. And love is what life is all about.

It really all comes down to the Golden Rule. Luke 6:31 NIV says, "Do to others as you would have them do to you." Consider your past arguments. Now consider if others treated you the way they wanted to be treated. Guess what? You get to be the solution. It has to start somewhere, and you are the one to bring that love revolution to your world!

Chapter 7

Character

Becoming a Person of Love

Character is what you are made of. Your character shows up when you are hit hard—not when life is easy. Are you honest, faithful, loyal, kind, giving, and loving? Are you greedy, prideful, arrogant, stingy, and mean? Or are you a mixture of all these qualities? Sometimes we know who we are, and sometimes we surprise even ourselves in both positive and negative ways. Often, the most accurate account of who we really are, outside of our blind spots, comes from others' perceptions. I'm not talking about just anyone but those who really know you and are invested in your life.

Ask three to five of the closest people in your life to share with you what they perceive as your strengths. Do they see any blind spots? Then I challenge you to compare notes with the feedback you receive. When you see a recurring word, trait, or circumstance, pay close attention to it. Ask the Lord how you can use this strength for Him and how you can overcome your weakness. You can take small steps; they will lead to big change.

Another simple way to see how your characteristics are affecting those around you is to ask yourself some questions. You can ask the Holy Spirit to help you see:

1. How do others react to me? (Are they intimidated, validated, freed, or forgotten?)
2. Do people seem interested in what I have to say?
3. Do people ask me for advice, or is my opinion on things important to them?
4. Do people confide in or trust me?
5. Do people care about me and my vision?
6. Do I recognize when people have something important to deal with and need to get away?
7. Do I find myself speaking negatively about others?
8. Do I find myself really celebrating others' successes?

Awareness of your character and how others perceive you is a really important quality. If you have the most valuable message to bring but you are misperceived, it could stop your entire message from being heard, resulting in a detrimental outcome. On the other hand, if you remain teachable by caring enough to learn about the different methods of communication and choosing to honor others by communicating in a way they can receive it, then your message will be heard.

Chances are that you will not be liked by everyone, but you can love everyone. The more people you are exposed to the greater the number of people who will not like you. That is okay. You can still choose to be aware of the state of those you are interacting with and respond in love to their reactions. Someone who spends energy being aware of others is a person with love at the foundation of his or her character.

One important aspect of dealing with others is to remember that you do not know what they are going through. You do not know what their journey has held or why they may perceive you the way they do. Just be who you are; be the person you have decided to be. Don't worry about others seeing you as perfect. If they are offended by who you are, even if you aren't wrong, it's okay to apologize for their experience of you. You can follow that up by inviting them to get to know the real you. If you remain loyal, kind, gentle, loving, merciful, trustworthy, and present, you will become a model of benevolent behavior. Others will want to be more like the person they see you growing into. They will see your peace and want it. Loving in the face of being rejected or misunderstood marks a person of great character. I believe you have what it takes to be that type of person.

Chapter 8

About Pride

Deflating Your Ego

Pride almost always comes before a fall. What is pride?

> noun
> a high or inordinate opinion of one's own dignity, importance, merit, or superiority, whether as cherished in the mind or as displayed in bearing, conduct, etc. *http://dictionary.reference.com/browse/pride*

Pride is thinking you are better than someone else. Pride involves feeling entitled. Pride requires acknowledgment and often demands it if it's not freely offered. Pride makes the world—your world—all about *you*. Pride puffs up your sense of importance, your requirements, and your need for attention. Sadly, pride often disables your ability to truly love and/or be loved. Pride debilitates your capacity to recognize and meet the needs of others. Pride causes you to rarely think about others if at all. And when you do, you somehow have to think negatively about them to continue holding yourself up. I dare say that pride is the opposite of love and grace.

I have weathered a few crises and encountered a good deal of turmoil in my life thus far. My parents moved us seventeen times before I was eighteen years old; through their journey, they went bankrupt twice. They died two years apart from cancer, each at sixty-two years of age. I have been an adrenaline junky, endangering my life and the lives of others many times. I have dealt with family members and friends with mental illnesses. When I was a volunteer firefighter, I witnessed lives being torn apart and many deaths. Through every crisis, I typically responded with cool calmness and tried to fix or improve each situation.

Over time, I started thinking I had this little red cape that made me better than most people. I tried not to show those feelings, but I'm sure people around me got a glimpse of the exaggerated opinions I had about myself. I would tell people that all my success and strength came from God, which I somewhat believed, but there were still flaws in my self-image. Before the real estate market crashed, I prayed that God would do whatever it took to make me into what He wanted me to be. I don't think I knew what I was actually praying for or what it would entail. But He took full advantage of that prayer. I also told myself that I only had one chance at life, and I was going to try and take our company, Global, well, *global.*

I wanted our company to be the number-one source in the world for investment and vacation property. We were making money hand over fist, and I was buying investment properties faster than the money was coming in. In fact, I got so aggressive in buying that I disregarded the agreement Robyn and I had made to pray and agree beforehand about any purchases. She had a tendency to see the risks in opportunities, while I tended to see only the benefits. On a couple of opportunities, we were not in agreement, but I went ahead and did the deals. This in turn put stress on our marriage and set me up for disaster. I made excuses for my decisions under the guise of doing what was best for our family and others. I told myself that I could use a lot of the additional profits to help those in need.

In this same time period, we also opened our third office and spent a fortune to make it into a masterpiece. But in the fall of 2005, our sales basically stopped. We were primarily selling properties to foreign investors, and some stopped paying their mortgages when they were unable sell the properties. This led the banks to stop lending. The lack of money available for lending was detrimental to the business of flipping newly-constructed homes. There were no more approved buyers. A couple years later, the financial and credit crisis came. This series of economic events caused our income to drop by 80 to 90 percent. We owed more on most of our investments than they were worth.

Contrary to my naturally cheerful disposition, these events triggered my slide into depression. I had allowed money to become so important that it was affecting my mental health. I became painfully aware that I wasn't the Christian I thought I was. The potter, God, knew that I, the pot, had flaws. He allowed my flawed self to shatter on the floor so that He could rebuild me. Hopefully this time, the clay would cooperate and let the heavenly potter shape him to reflect the His workmanship.

That process is what it took to work pride out of our lives. Pride almost always comes before we fall. In other words, our puffed up state of pride will always get deflated. When we entertain how much better we are than others and how much more we deserve, we are positioning ourselves to be blindsided by hardship. It is far better to admit how much we need God and ask Him to lead, guide, and direct our steps.

Unfortunately, most of us have to learn this lesson the hard way (at least once) to grasp its magnitude. Being humbled by God, however, is really an act of His love—not rejection.

> The burden in your heart will begin to lift.

If you are going through a terrible storm, you can choose to shoulder through it by your own strength. Maybe you'll come out on the other side battered, torn, and bitter. Or, like me, maybe you'll come through thinking you are superman.

But there is another choice. You can seek God in the middle of your storm. You can realize that you do not have everything you need apart from Him. Admit your need for Him, and ask for help. With that request, I can guarantee that even if your storm doesn't lift, the burden in your heart will begin to. The storm within you will subside as peace and calm enter in. You will find that your mind becomes clearer, and you will begin to think of others more than yourself. It will be the start of something beautiful.

But why wait for a storm? Today can be the day you decide to stop going at this big, burdensome life thing alone. Even if you are prospering financially, it means nothing if your soul is dying. Unfortunately for most of us, when we are prosperous, we can have a false sense of being invincible. But money is just paper. Who you are is where your true wealth is. Apart from your finances, how are you? Who are you? Could you use some help? Could you use some freedom? What about peace or joy? Today is the perfect day to humble yourself, pray, and ask God to help you.

It could be as simple as praying this:

> Jesus, somehow along the way, I bought the message that I had to figure life out on my own. But that is only working in some aspects of my life. I would like to invite You into my life, including the parts that seem to be working and the parts that are noticeably broken. I admit this day that I need You. Will You give me wisdom, guidance, and direction? Will You teach me Your ways and help me see others and myself as You see us? Thank You ahead of time, Lord, for Your kindness toward me. In Jesus's name I pray, amen.

Chapter 9

On Finances

Spending, Saving, and Giving

A few years ago, I was on a church advisory board. One service we offered was meeting with people who wanted financial help from the church. The first thing we would have them do was make a budget. About 90 percent of them had more money going out than coming in each month, which surprised them. The first step to achieving financial well-being is to create a monthly budget. Make the cuts you have to in order to live within your means. It may mean cutting cable television service, eating at home more often, wearing clothes you already own instead of buying new ones, and so forth.

It may seem hard at first, but I can promise you that the stress you avoid will be more than worth it. I have spent most of my career in sales. As my income went up so did my spending. I would find myself living paycheck to paycheck or even going into debt no matter how much I made. I had a dream car, a pair of jet skis, and a boat. But I learned that those possessions only created a burden. Stuff does not bring happiness; it actually increases stress because it needs maintenance and gas and the list just goes on. I actually found peace in spending less and simplifying my tastes.

Another important reason to simplify is because life is full of different seasons—even financial ones. I would have a season of abundance and overspend instead of save. Then I would come into a dry season a little behind, which increased the difficulty of navigating through the dry spell. Now I have learned that when I am in a season of plenty, it's wise to put some of the extra away because there will always be another dry season. I do not have to fear it; I just need to be prepared for it.

> God doesn't need your money.

Finally, I wanted to touch on giving. Giving really has to do with the condition of your heart. Giving is proof of your belief in God. If you believe in Him and recognize Him as your provider, then you know it is true that all money is His. Also, it is important to recognize that God doesn't need your money. He requires giving from us because He wants to see that our faith is composed of more than words.

The first step in giving is to ask God to grow a spirit of generosity in you. The next step is to find something you believe in supporting, and start giving there. One of the most rewarding aspects of giving is how it keeps your life in proper perspective in terms of what is going on in the world. Remembering that others have needs you can meet will keep you working with purpose. It will also help you avoid self-pity or depression when you hit a bump in the road. Giving is for you as much as it is for those you are giving to. You will find tremendous blessing in giving with a happy heart.

Here are a few quick tips toward financial freedom.

1. Make and keep a budget.
    a. Spend less than you make each month. Cut whatever you have to in order to make this happen.
    b. It is okay if you don't have the latest of everything.
    c. Wait until you can pay cash, and then enjoy the purchases.
2. Be aware of different financial seasons.
    a. You will probably experience seasons of plenty and seasons of want.
    b. In a season of plenty, put some extra funds aside to prepare for future seasons.
    c. Don't go into debt in seasons of plenty by spending potential income before you actually make it.
3. Give.
    a. Ask God to create in you a generous spirit.
    b. Giving will keep your life connected to the whole world.
    c. Giving will help you keep going when times are difficult.
    d. Give to something you believe in and feel passionate about.

Chapter 10

What's the Upside?
Powerful Decision Making

We were on a family vacation with close friends in Jamaica. While we headed for a waterfall that was mostly visited by locals, our friends' teenage son was embracing his free spirit by climbing trees, running through the jungle, and exploring the surrounding nature. In his explorations, he happened upon a cliff. The next thing I knew, he took a long running start and flew through the air. He landed about five feet from the base of the rock that he jumped from. It looked fun, really fun, and I wanted it to be my turn next. In all honesty, I have always enjoyed adrenaline rushes and showing off, so I began climbing to the top of the cliff and prepared to jump. Then something unexpected happened. For the first time in my life in this type of situation, I asked myself the question: *What is the upside versus the downside?*

I was about forty years old when I asked myself that question. It took forty years before I really stopped to assess pros versus cons in a dangerous situation. Before then, the thrill of showing my wild side, pushing myself to the edge of my abilities, and experiencing the rush of adrenaline had always overshadowed any possible negative consequences.

So for the first time, I thoughtfully contemplated the cons. They included how I could get hurt if I didn't clear the bottom of the rocky slope. I could break bones in the middle of a Jamaican jungle—a long, bumpy bus ride away from the nearest hospital. That possibility didn't excite me. On the other hand, if I jumped successfully, I would get a brief adrenaline rush and show off for my family and friends. I determined the possible cost wasn't worth the thrill. I didn't take the pointless risk, and I thoroughly enjoyed the rest of my Jamaican vacation—unharmed. I didn't even entertain thoughts about what I *missed* by choosing not to jump.

> Become intentional about the choices you make.

The funny thing about it is that you never know when you are experiencing a life-changing moment. That event remains crystal clear in my memory because it was a turning point in my decision making process. From that moment on, I began to apply careful logic to decisions I made and advice I gave to others.

Don't make decisions without thinking about the downside and taking it to God in prayer. A lot of poor choices or regrets in life have been made in haste, with little or no consideration of what risks we were allowing into our lives. Quality choices are ones made without urgency, with a lot of prayer, and with wise council from trusted voices around us—people who have lived longer, experienced more, and have similar morals and goals. I have had the joy and honor of being on both sides of this relationship.

One topic I can counsel others on happens to be business. When friends ask me if they should start a business, I begin helping them by weighing the risks involved against the possible benefits. I can help in this arena because I have been building businesses all of my life. Wisdom comes with that type of experience. I am able to gauge the reality of what a business will require, what it will cost, and what it will produce. Here is a glimpse into my decision process when it comes to start-ups.

Pros:
You can possibly gain financial freedom and prestige. You can experience being your own boss.

Cons:
You will have to give up your current stable job. For at least the first five to ten years, there will be an incredible amount of stress, which you are unacquainted with if this is your first time building and running a company. You also have to consider that there is always the potential for failure and financial meltdown.

I have started several businesses over the years, but I tell people that if I knew *then* what I know *now*, I probably wouldn't have started them. I thank God that it has worked out so far, but it is much wiser to approach decisions logically instead of emotionally.

Here are some key thoughts to help you gain a better relationship with decision-making.

1. Am I feeling pressured to make this decision quickly? (*Stop!*)
2. Have I prayed about it? (If you haven't, don't make a move until you do.)
3. What have my mentors shared with me about this idea?
4. If I weren't feeling _____ (insert emotion), would my choice still be the same?
5. What is the upside (pros, benefits, possible good outcomes)?
6. What is the downside (cons, prohibitive costs, possible negative effects)?

You owe it to yourself and your future to become intentional about the choices you make. Life isn't happening to you. You are choosing the type of life you get to experience. If you aren't happy with your current progress, try making some better-quality decisions. *You have what it takes!* There is a bright future ahead of you. Believe it, and make choices that take you in that direction!

Chapter 11

Work Hard and Good Things Will Happen
Excellence vs. Greed

I will never regret working for my dreams. They mainly consist of helping people around the world and enjoying more of earth's blessings. I am not afraid to work hard to accomplish and enjoy all that I long to experience. However, I am beginning to see a trend in the generations coming up behind me. Many resent having to work hard to get the results they want in their lives. Somewhere along the way, we have raised a generation of young people who think everyone else owes them what they want.

You are responsible for creating the life you want. No one owes you anything. Work hard, dream big, serve others, and you will find yourself fulfilled.

A former pastor of mine used to say that if you have an old car, take great care of it, and God may bless you with a nicer car. If you shovel poop for a living, be the best poop scooper in the world. Colossians 3:23 NIV says,

> Whatever you do, work at it with all your heart,
> as working for the Lord, not for human masters.

What an encouraging change in perspective. Instead of working hard for the boss or parent or spouse who doesn't appreciate us, let's work for the Lord with all that we have to give. Allow Him to promote us as He sees fit. He has given us everything, and we can never repay Him. The least we can do is give back to Him by obeying His commandments and living by a standard of excellence.

Excellence is the exact opposite of doing what I have to do—of just getting by. Excellence means asking how to do something better, more effectively, more efficiently, and with more effort than I am paid for. How can I create and add value to this relationship by serving it with my whole heart? How can I bless the company I work for by doing this better than expected? That is excellence. If you possess that mentality and work ethic, the Lord will bless you abundantly!

> Excellence is the exact opposite of doing just what I have to do.

I have experienced this principle of working with excellence and watched it play out in the lives of others. For example, my kids have friends who received expensive new cars in their teenage years. Since they did not have to earn their luxurious car, they did not appreciate the value of what they had been given. Many didn't maintain their cars properly; as a result, their cars had short lives. Conversely, teenagers who started out with clunkers and took pride in them ended up driving nice cars that are valued and well cared for. Sometimes giving people something they didn't have to work for can damage their ability to appreciate its value. If someone I love wants something, I give that person the opportunity to earn it. When people have "skin in the game," they just care more.

Some of the people we hire for entry-level positions go above and beyond the call of duty. They add more value to our company. As a result, we promote them to top management positions in our organization. When someone cares, it shows.

It's important to take pride in everything you have been given, acknowledging the value and worth it has in your life. If you honor what you have been given, there is a good chance that even greater things will happen to you and for you.

There is another aspect of this principle. To really enjoy achievements in life, you need to work with integrity. It is important not to compromise yourself in an attempt to improve your situation. A leader in our last church told me he had found a great way to make some extra money; he was burning custom CDs for people and selling them. This was actual piracy and definitely illegal.

Any time you think you need to do something illegal to make ends meet, you have somehow stopped believing that God is your ultimate provider. If you confess that you love God and receive His love, then you trust that He will put the opportunities in front of you that He wants you to pursue. They won't be illegal or immoral.

However, I fully believe that such opportunities arise to help us clarify the decisions we make. Our choices at these crossroads reveal what is truly in our hearts. Actions speak louder than words.

I've personally had opportunities to cut corners to make extra money or cover up a mistake or oversight. There are times when I could've cheated to make extra money here or there. But I had to trust God completely.

No matter how much money is at stake, if you must do something wrong to make money, then pass on it. Greed will never make you happy. You will never be able to satisfy that appetite, and you can potentially hurt everyone you love if you pursue it. However, if you stay the course by choosing the way of integrity, I'm betting that a better opportunity will come along. Who knows? Maybe the better one wouldn't show up if you took the first one.

Here are some things to ponder.

1. Do I think someone else should give me what I want?
2. Am I afraid to work hard?
3. Do I consider that I'm doing everything for the Lord alone?
4. Will I work with a heart-based attitude of excellence?
5. Has greed caused me to compromise integrity?
6. Is there anything I have been freely given that I need to appreciate more?

Chapter 12

Being Humble
Recognizing Grace

Humility is a great quality. It comes easier to some than others. In my experience, humility has come from the revelation that I deserve nothing. It's only by God's grace that I have anything—including my gifting, talents, relationships, and every good thing in my life. Recently, we had some big victories at work, and a couple of people said, "Congratulations! You deserve this!" I replied, "I don't deserve anything!"

Their expressions told me that they thought I was portraying false humility; in reality, I believe that I don't deserve anything. Only by the grace of God have I been given the opportunity to share in His glory.

I did nothing to deserve life, but I can give out of the bounty of my life. I could have been born into extreme poverty. I could have been born with any number of physical, emotional, or relational challenges greater than what I have experienced. It would be totally arrogant and completely wrong to think that I am fully responsible for my health and ability to love, learn, and overcome.

I need to fully recognize that God gives me the gifts that help me succeed. God puts the opportunities in front of me. The only thing I deserve credit for is seeking His guidance and trying to follow His path. Understanding this makes it impossible to be arrogant.

Another result of a humble attitude is that you will find yourself inclined toward a thankful—as opposed to a bitter—attitude. If you find yourself bitter about your life and the way it has turned out, you need to humble yourself and ask God to show you what is right. Focus on what you have, and give thanks for it. One of my favorite quotations is, "Out of any opportunity you can become bitter or better; it's your choice." It is never fun to be around a bitter person who blames others for his or her problems. It's up to you to make the best out of the hand you are dealt.

During a period of life when the Lord was teaching me humility and draining me of pride, we maxed out every credit line and equity line we had. There was a real possibility that we would never take a nice vacation again and that we would have to work until we died. I also thought we might lose our personal residence and possibly the business, but I became reconciled with all that. I knew I had grabbed the steering wheel of my life, and I had a crashed and burned. I repented for being a bad steward of God's properties and asked Him to take the wheel. I knew then that I'd be happy going wherever He took me.

I did manage to set some goals during that season. I asked God to allow our youngest child to graduate high school before we lost the house to the bank. I don't remember the rest of my goals, but they were not very lofty. In that state, dreaming big seemed to elude me. But I knew God would get glory no matter the result. I chose to admit I was wrong, asked for help, and trusted Him to bring whatever outcome He desired.

As a result of those choices and God's favor, our business is now doing better than before the economic crisis. And I wouldn't trade the tribulation for anything. Because I walked through that hard, painful, and scary season, I'm a different person. Hopefully, I am a better Christian, husband, father, and friend.

One of the benefits of pursuing humility is escaping the pressure of being perfect or getting it right all the time. When you aren't preoccupied with that expectation, you are free to admit a mistake, apologize, and ask for forgiveness.

Saying sorry is something I can't seem to wear out. I am happy to be the first one to apologize. It doesn't matter what I am sorry about; simply apologizing always helps diffuse a troublesome situation. I am okay with making a mistake. When I recognize it or when someone else calls me on it, I can admit it and make changes to be in the right again.

> Escape the pressure of getting it right all of the time.

The deepest gift of humility is the quickness with which you learn your lesson and become free to move forward. Allowing the Lord to humble you simply means keeping your eyes on Him and off yourself. You recognize everything He has given you; you could never deserve it all. Be intentional about giving thanks for His gifts and serving Him through those gifts. You will never regret seeking a humble heart!

Chapter 13

Nothing Good Happens after Midnight
Choosing Healthy Relationships

Have you ever found yourself out late at night, changing the world for the better? How about impacting someone's life in a good way? Or handling yourself in a way you would want the whole world to see? My guess is, probably not.

It remains consistently true in my life that nothing good comes of being out past midnight—the hours when men and women often get together. With guards down and clouded judgment, they make choices that will not benefit themselves or others. Most of the time, such decisions bring pain, heartache, and suffering.

When my kids were getting older, they kept pushing me to allow them to stay out later and later. I told them that if they wanted to have more time with their friends, they could wake up earlier and enjoy their company during the day. That is a parenting choice I celebrate without regret. They did not miss out on anything beneficial by being home late at night and neither will you.

I have been writing about a specific time frame, but let's explore this topic a little deeper. I would also suggest not hanging around those who won't lift you up when you are vulnerable in some way—tired, down, overwhelmed, or in need of a break. Who you choose to be around when you are vulnerable can really impact your future journey.

Jesus had twelve disciples He walked with on the earth. Three He allowed to observe the deeper aspects of His life. I believe this is a good model to follow. Who in your life is there to stretch, challenge, encourage, and believe in you? Who really knows who you are and where you are headed? If you aren't clear yet on your life's course, who could help you discover who you are and what you were made for? Who is there to call you out when you want to give up?

The people who come to mind are your three. You need those three when you are in your midnight hour, when everything seems dark. This one choice can change everything else for you, including your future impact on the world.

Don't wait until midnight to make the choices you see successful people making. Wise choices don't happen haphazardly. They happen on purpose. You too can determine to make the changes you desire for your life. If you want to stop positioning yourself for defeat and drawbacks, choose now. Take a look at the areas you want to grow in or feel defeated by, and write them down. Take some time to pray. Ask God to show you how to purposefully enjoy the change you desire. Write down the strategy. Don't wait until the darkness sets in; that is not the time to try it out. Begin now.

Victory can be yours. You really can make those changes and enjoy the life you dream of. Believe it or not, no one else can do this for you. You can replace the destructive cycles that have kept you stuck for so long with constructive cycles that will catapult you forward. Start with one at a time. Stick to the change; once it's a nonissue, add to it. Before you know it, not only will you be enjoying the life you've longed for but you will be helping others do the same!

Here's a quick review of the questions to ponder and pray about.

1. Who are the three people in my life who are safe to be around when I have an emotional need?
2. What areas of my life keep me feeling defeated, stuck, or hopeless?
3. What is a practical strategy I can implement, little by little, to overcome this destructive pattern?
4. What will try to stop me, and how will I stick to my new normal?
5. How will it feel to really live on purpose and enjoy being free in this area?
6. How will I celebrate my successful change?

Chapter 14

Unforgiveness

Letting Go

Everyone has baggage. Some of the most lethal baggage I have carried around is unforgiveness.

The truth is that we will all offend each other at some point. Sometimes we will be the offenders, and sometimes we will be the ones who are offended. It is very valuable to know how to navigate through choices, moments, actions, and words that require forgiveness.

The first step toward choosing forgiveness is to rid yourself of the victim mentality. If you consistently view the person causing you harm as your attacker or abuser (even if it is true), you won't be positioned for victory. The victory never goes to the victim. So how can you change your perspective?

Perspectives only change by making a choice to change. You have to decide that carrying around your unforgiveness hasn't worked for you so far. You have to consider where you want to go and whether or not you can get there with all the dead weight of unforgiveness. You see, forgiveness isn't even about the other guy. It is truly about loving, valuing, and honoring yourself.

I have heard it said that unforgiveness is like drinking poison and then waiting for it to hurt the other person in the conflict. In reality, you are choosing to poison your own soul by holding on to whatever negative emotion you have attached to that specific memory.

In the early days of my marriage, Robyn and I both felt unforgiveness toward each other. This feeling eventually morphed into resentment. To move forward together, we had to better understand love. We realized that we loved each other; we chose to accept each other's strengths and weaknesses. We knew this revelation came as a result of seeking God for solutions to the problems we faced. Once the Lord revealed that my heart was wrong, I had to make a decision to turn away from that and turn toward what He said was true about my wife.

> Forgiveness is about loving yourself.

I am so thankful that I learned to ask God to search my heart and show me what was steering me off the life path I was created to follow. This request has been a huge gift to me over and over again.

If this is something you want to try, you can pray this prayer:

> Search me, God, and know my heart;
> test me and know my anxious thoughts.
> See if there is any offensive way in me,
> and lead me in the way everlasting. Psalm 139:23–24 NIV

Then, as you go about your day, you will become more aware of how often you are offended. You will also become more aware of your thoughts toward and about others. You will even find that your word choices are amplified in your own ears.

As you awaken to a new awareness about yourself, the invitation comes to turn from the things that are hurting you or others. You can then replace them with beneficial mindsets, words, reactions, and beliefs. Opportunities will open up to forgive, let go, and return to love. As a result, you will even start liking yourself more, which will affect how you treat others.

Chapter 15

People Pleasing

Overcoming Fear of Rejection

People pleasing parades itself around as love but is never really love. It may appear as pure, selfless actions, yet there is usually an agenda attached to such behavior. When we work hard to please everyone around us, our motives are typically impure. We are either afraid of rejection if we don't make others happy, or we must keep others happy for some benefit they offer us in return. For example, some people tiptoe around those with money (like grandparents or parents) to ensure that they aren't cut off from financial help. Others do whatever they feel is expected of them, even if it's not what they feel called to do or are passionate about. In that case, their fear of rejection is greater than their sense of identity.

People pleasing can permeate any type of relationship. I have seen this behavior cost people their jobs, reputations, hopes, dreams, and even their marriages. Many people feel the pressure to please their spouses with material things. The result is that they end up letting their spouses overspend. This happens when one partner is afraid to share his or her true financial burdens or stress in order to keep the other partner happy. Unfortunately, these choices end up putting more stress on the relationship.

I recommend praying about every financial decision and considering personal motives. My love for my wife makes me want to please her; this desire can lead me make the wrong decision with the right motivation. If I really love her, I will respect her by sharing the truth with her and protecting our long-term goals by not spending more than we currently have.

> Is your fear of rejection greater than your sense of identity?

There are more examples of people pleasing that extend beyond marriage.

- Parents want to please their children so much that they forget to be parents.
- People in ministry want to please others so much that they burn out and end up disillusioned, hurt, and weary.
- Young people try to please their boyfriends or girlfriends and end up compromising their hopes, dreams, and destinies to give in those who have not yet committed their lives to them.
- Employees long to be so pleasing to their bosses that they forgot about their personal lives and end up losing everyone they truly care about.

Whatever the scenario, the result is the same—people pleasing out of fear of rejection or loss of personal benefit never ends well. So how can we detect it? What can we do about it?

First of all, it's important to for us to really know that we are all created with a unique plan and purpose for our lives. We need to know that God is real. He is alive, and He completely knows us. He fully accepts us. And His approval is real; it's not approval based on us, it is based on Him. In light of this total and utter acceptance, when we experience the sting of rejection—and live through it just a few times—we discover that it really isn't so bad. It's surely nothing to fear.

Next, we have to decide who we are, have a clear direction, and define our goals and purposes. Begin believing in ourselves and in who God says we are regardless of what others believe about us. By doing this self-work, we will see a dramatic change in how people relate to us. Some people will reject our new assertive selves, especially those who are used to who we used to be— the ones who would say yes to any request. In contrast, the relationships we form or improve on after this self-work will be vibrant and rich because we will be free to be oursleves. Relationships won't end if we displease people or they displease us. We are committed and will work through the problem to find a resolution and move forward.

Lastly, we will begin to establish clear boundaries—what we are willing to invest in each relationship. A healthy approach to boundary setting is to evaluate our motives. Why do we want to give the person this gift? Is our decision based on a true willingness, or are we afraid of what will happen if we do not do it? By taking the time to become aware of our relational motives, we can begin living above rather than under fear. We will then experience healthy, symbiotic relationships instead of relationships with emotionally abusive tendencies. We will notice the people we are surrounding ourselves with are the kind of people who value and respect the real people we are becoming. We will begin to believe in who we have been created to be. And we will dare to believe that our purposes can be achieved.

Once these changes take place, we will be better equipped to love well. The people who really matter in our lives—the ones who are in our intentional communities—will reap the greatest benefit from our hard inner work. They will begin to see how much we value them, how much we value ourselves, and the possibility of a future they might have stopped hoping for long ago.

We are not the victims of the people around us. Change is possible. Let's begin finding out today who we really are, where we are headed, how we are going to get there, and what we need to overcome along the way. Remember: we are fully known and fully loved. We are fully accepted as we are on the way to where we are going. We do not need to fear rejection. We have been created with a plan and purpose. No is an acceptable answer to a request or a favor. It is okay to be and continually become ourselves.

Chapter 16

Accountability
Living Authentically

One essential aspect of truly becoming a person who thrives and makes quality choices is having people to whom you are accountable. Your closest friends should be people you can trust with the ups and downs of your life. However, your friends may not be among the select few to hold you accountable in your pursuit of becoming who you want to be. If you don't know where to find accountability, I recommend that you pray and ask God to bring people with that purpose to you. Look for people who possess the characteristics you wish to possess such as purpose, integrity, love, wisdom, or patience.

With accountability comes sharing our struggles with others. The truth is that we all struggle with sin, and sin can't survive in the light. When we let it out or confess it to someone trustworthy and loving, we experience refreshment and relief. The burden of carrying the guilt of secret sin is enough to destroy anyone. But once sin is confessed, we experience the desire to turn toward God and receive His forgiveness. This is an exchange from shame to hope, distress to peace, and pain to purpose.

Most of us believe that our failures are worse than everyone else's. We believe that if people actually knew what we have done, they would no longer love us. That is not the truth. God already knows what has transpired in our hearts and in our actions, and He still loves us. His forgiveness is available to us always.

When we understand that God loves us and wants the best for us, we can then bring our shame to Him through accountability. But it can be harder to ask for accountability in the areas where we experience the most shame. Yet, we need to address these areas the most.

For example, one struggle that can feel particularly shameful is the struggle with pornography. This is one of the most prevalent sins in our society today. When I was in my early twenties, my pastor gave me a book on pornography written by C. Everett Coop, the US Surgeon General at the time. Referring to a study conducted at major universities, Coop explained how viewing pornography affected one's ability to connect, value, and have viable relationships with women.

The study had groups of people view either cartoons or pornography. The group that watched pornography began to see women in a different light. They viewed them more as sex objects, things to be used rather than human beings to know. This included the women who watched pornography. A lot of them felt that when a woman was saying no, she really meant yes. They also learned that people who watched large amounts of pornography started with traditional sex, but over time, they watched more deviant material to become stimulated. Have you wondered why some predators are obsessed with children? It's a slippery slope that leads straight to hell.

If you can't shake this demon, there are resources available to you. You can find a group and get help. Confess to someone. Put accountability software on your computer such as *www.xxxchurch.com*. This hidden sin will cost you more than you think and cause you to hurt others.

Pornography is one of many sins we believe we can't reveal to others. Many things plague us secretly. Maybe you are binge eating, cutting yourself, feeling depressed but pretending to be happy, or are involved in an adulterous affair. Perhaps there is hatred in your heart for someone who has hurt you. Maybe you believe that your life is perfect, but you don't care about anyone but yourself. Whatever plagues you is not bigger than God. He forgives you as you turn away from sin and toward Him. He restores you and works everything together for good.

> Whatever plagues you is not bigger than God.

So what does it look like to have an accountability partner? Or how can you surround yourself with people who hold each another accountable? For me, accountability has looked different during different life seasons. If I had certain destructive cycles I needed to break through, my accountability would be more intentional in those seasons. I confessed my desire to break free and asked certain people to help me walk through that season. I composed questions that I wanted to be asked weekly at pre-arranged times—hard questions addressing my area of struggle. Since I knew someone would ask me those questions, I had plenty of motivation to stay on track. But when I fell, I could stand back up again quickly because I had someone to help me look at the cycle, determine why I fell, and plan a strategy to avoid repeating that particular slip. I believe it truly takes community effort to achieve and maintain a victorious life.

In other seasons, I have been around likeminded people—those with similar goals and heart attitudes. When something was amiss with me, these invested friends asked me questions from a place of concern. They might say, "That doesn't sound like you; is everything okay?" or "I've noticed you have been _____ lately; what's going on?" or remind me, "Hey, remember that time you were so passionate about _____? How is that going?" Then they'd take the time to listen as I shared. And when I felt genuinely heard and cared about, I found the courage to open up to them.

Accountability is not only beneficial when trying to overcome an obstacle, it is also beneficial when striving toward goals or pursuing passions. Having others to remind you of *why* you are doing *what* you are doing will stimulate growth. It is important to be surrounded by people who believe you can do it and who will help you up when you fall. Really, we need accountability in every aspect of our lives. We need to open up and express our need for each other. We need to be there for others and invite them to be there for us. We are truly better, stronger, braver, and victorious together!

So, who can hold you accountable? Who needs you? Whom do you need? What aspect of your life could benefit from accountability? Are there any destructive cycles you need to break free of? Is there any particular goal you can't seem to obtain on your own? I encourage you to spend some time considering these questions. This is your life. You do not get another one. And one way to make it count is to intentionally and authentically do life with others!

Chapter 17

Show Me Your Friends, and I'll Show You Your Future

Intentional Relationships

None of us surrounds ourselves with people by accident. We may not get to choose who our family is, but we surely choose those with whom we do life. We choose our spouses and our friends. We choose how much of ourselves to invest in each relationship—the quantity and quality of time and emotion we give to each relationship. And it is impossible not to be impacted by someone who spends a significant amount of time with us.

Over the years, my kids probably got sick of this adage: "Show me your friends, and I'll show you your future." The minute I began to notice a change of behavior in them (for better or for worse), I would look for any change in friendships. My children have strong personalities; they are leaders. But even leaders are affected by those around them. I wanted to know who was impacting their thinking, attitudes, actions, and emotions.

The truth is that birds of a feather really do flock together. If you want to be successful, you should hang around people who work hard and have goals and ambition. The same principle applies if you want to be happy. Choose to hang around people who exude positive attitudes and who like to laugh. Adversely, if you want to end up in jail, surround yourself with takers and drug addicts. If you want to be miserable, find people who blame others for all their problems and never face the responsibility of their own actions and their own lives.

People come into our lives for different reasons and for different seasons. They can be your peers, friends, and mentors; some are there for you to mentor. These seasons and roles are ever changing, but it is wise to always have a mentor. This is someone who advises and gives counsel to help you navigate life with greater wisdom. I recommend praying and asking God to bring a mentor into your life if you do not already have one. I highly recommend that this person be at least a decade older than you and that you see evidence in his or her life of what you desire for your own life.

It's also important that you add value to the life of your mentor. When you enter into a relationship and take, take, take, burnout can happen. And if your mentor ends the relationship, you may receive that termination as rejection. To protect the relationship—and love each other well—you need to be appreciative of the time and energy your mentor extends to you. Saying thank you goes a long way. Also, heeding your mentor's wisdom and sharing your victories will fuel your mentor's desire to continue investing in your life.

Your mentor and other people can be a great source of happiness. If you are not in agreement with the majority of those around you, then you need to reevaluate why you attract people who are not inspiring you. Do you believe you possess enough worth and value to be friends with people who inspire you? You do. You are enough.

Are you afraid of people who possess more than you currently have? Are you allowing intimidation to steal the possibility of great relationships? Or do you perhaps surround yourself with people who feel inferior so that you can feel superior? Whatever your relationships are, it is good to evaluate why you have chosen them, the dynamics of each relationship, and if there is any room for growth or maturity on your part.

It is wise to invite a combination of people into your life. You need those who are not afraid to point out where you can make improvements. You also need those who give you positive reinforcement when you are heading in the right direction.

I always value people who are praying for me and will share a message from God, even if they know I might not want to hear it. Something is probably out of balance if the people in your life are only either corrective or encouraging. We need both correction and encouragement, and we should extend the same to others.

What do you want out of relationships? Hopefully, it is congruent with what you want to give to them. I want to be inspired, and I want to inspire. I want to be around people who are better parents, better business people, and better at following and serving Christ than I am. I also want to be involved in lives where I can be the one with experience to share. I want people to show me things about myself that I don't see, and I want to help them recognize their blind spots and gifts. Lastly, I want people to love me and embrace who I am today, on the way to where I am going. And I want to extend that grace to others on their journeys along their way.

The majority of the people who are close to me are working toward similar goals. I have friends who care about others and who want to be successful by helping, loving, and giving. I surround myself with people I admire and who I can be honest with. My friends are willing to enjoy life and fight for the lives of those who are hurting. They are people I can grow with. My friends are not competing against me. Our dreams are bigger than ourselves. And our hearts have found unity. When I look at my friends right now, I like what my future looks like. How about you?

Here are some questions to ponder.

1. Who are the people I am currently pouring my time, energy, and emotion into?
2. How did I choose these relationships?
3. What is my goal for these connections? Am I willing to give as much as I take? Are others willing to give to me as much as they take from me?
4. Where are my friends going? Is that where I want to end up?
5. Are the people in my life fighting next to me for a cause greater than themselves?
6. Do I need or want to have a mentor? Or is there anyone in my life whom I can intentionally mentor?

Chapter 18

Marriage

Loving Others More Than Yourself

As of the writing of this book, my wife and I have just celebrated our twenty-fifth wedding anniversary. It was such a joy to be surrounded by the people who have impacted and been impacted by our marriage and celebrate the love, commitment, and purpose Robyn and I have been able to enjoy and accomplish together. When I consider our marriage, I know that inviting God to be the center of our relationship has been the key to its success. But I would like to share a few other keys that have also proven successful in our lives.

Considering first things first, divorce is not an option. When we committed our lives to each other, my wife and I shared a mutual understanding that we were burning the bridge behind us and moving forward together in this world as one.

When you threaten to leave—or you actually do leave in the heat of the argument—the confidence you and your spouse have in your relationship dramatically decreases. If you are not working together toward a lifelong goal, then every aspect of your relationship will suffer. Conversely, if you are both aware of the vision, goal, and purpose of your relationship, then the trust, companionship, and love will increase through every circumstance.

Another critical skill has been the ability to throw water on fire. I've learned that when a disagreement erupts, I have some choices to make. If I want my wife to feel loved, I have to be sure I am fighting for something God wants for us. I have to check my motives and make sure I am not acting in a selfish manner. If I am, the fight will only cause harm to her and our relationship. If I don't get what I want in the moment but I still get to love and enjoy my beautiful wife, it is the real win.

Also, you might be amazed how something that seems so important can become a nonissue with just a night's sleep and some prayer. In a Bible study I attended years ago, I learned a way to pray using the acronym *ACTS*. It stands for adoration, confession, thanksgiving, and supplication. So when I pray, I begin with recognizing who God is. Next, I confess my sins and thank Him for His great love, forgiveness, lessons, and blessings. Then, I place my request before Him. Often, when I get to the part of voicing my complaint, it has become insignificant in light of who He is. I am reminded of what really matters and am able to let go of everything else. I have learned over the years that a praying husband has peace, love, joy, and satisfaction in marriage. He lives beside a wife who feels heard, seen, cherished, and valued. That is winning even when he doesn't *win* disagreements.

Another factor that has transformed our marriage has been choosing to focus on the positives in our relationship and on who we are as individuals. Earlier in my marriage, I had a mental image of what a perfect marriage looked like. I didn't appreciate the aspects of my marriage that didn't line up with that image. But now, I see how awful it would have been if God had given me what I thought I wanted. I so deeply appreciate the marriage He gave me.

Comparing your marriage to the marriages of others always leads to a negative result. Everyone is different. Focusing on the good God has given you always leads to positive results in your life. There is a lot of good right before you. Choose to see and celebrate what is right, good, desirable, and pleasing in your spouse and your marriage. The more you see and celebrate it the more it will increase.

> Comparing your marriage to other marriages always leads to a negative result.

As in all relationships, communication is crucial to a successful marriage. Sharing your feelings, expectations, hopes, and dreams with your spouse in a collaborative and honoring way is a very intimate and important aspect of loving each other. Expressing your need for one another and your delight in helping each other become who you were created to be matters. It's also important to create a safe place for each other to be vulnerable. Supporting each other in prayer, honesty, and active listening will produce an environment that propels you both forward in your purposes and fulfillment in life. That is a real treasure—one to pursue with all your heart.

Embrace the moment when your spouse shares a hurt with you. Choose not to become defensive or offended. A healthy relationship is one in which you do not have to withhold information from each other for fear of the spouse's reaction. When the exchange of negative emotions leads to an unhealthy outcome, each person begins to store up wounds. It's is the beginning of a rough time in marriage. If this has happened in your marriage, I encourage you to restore healthy communication by apologizing for how you responded in the past. It is important to reassure each other that you desire to listen with sensitivity and compassion. Work together toward a better outcome by making the choice to listen without giving offense and to shift, correct, and learn to respond with careful actions.

Lastly, enjoy the ride. We only get one time around this life journey, so we might as well enjoy it. Marriage is a lot of hard work, but there is no greater benefit than enjoying the fruit of all you have worked for.

Take vacations together. We have enjoyed many simple weekend getaways, which have deeply recharged our marriage. Celebrate milestones in ways that communicate how much you really see and know your spouse. If your wife loves expensive things and you hate spending money, buy her the expensive things she loves for her birthdays, anniversaries, and holidays. If it matters to her, do it even if it doesn't make sense to you. All these details matter. And your spouse is worth it. Your marriage and future are worth it.

To sum up, if you put the wants and desires of your spouse before your own, you will be blessed immensely.

Chapter 19

God's Promises

Perspective Shifts

A few years ago, I went through one of many periods of financial stress. We were planning to drive to Michigan to visit Robyn's family. Our company was small at the time, so I asked my accounting team (one person) how our cash flow looked. She informed me that we had $75,000 in bills and no money in the bank. We immediately canceled our travel plans. Since my credit cards were already maxed out, I had to borrow money from a friend just to survive. As you can imagine, it was a very stressful period. But I developed a perspective during that season that I still appreciate and use today.

Shortly before that period of time, I was playing with my son, Michael, in our backyard. Our pool has a retaining wall that is about ten feet above the backyard. Michael stood on the wall, facing the pool, with his back to our screen enclosure, which was rotten and falling apart. On one particular throw, I overshot, and the ball flew past Michael into the screen, causing a section to rip. My son ducked and fell face forward into a sharp plant. He then pulled away from the plant, grabbing the screen for support.

Unfortunately, he grabbed the section of screen that had just ripped. He tumbled out of our screen enclosure and off the ten-foot wall.

I panicked. I thought I had just killed my son. When I reached him, Michael was lying in the tall grass. Thank God, I hadn't mowed in a while! Michael was crying, but when he saw my face, he began crying even harder. What he saw was raw panic and misinterpreted it as anger. I knelt beside him to comfort him and noticed a grass stain on his head where he had hit the ground. I didn't pick him up at first because I was afraid he might have a spinal injury. I had him move his fingers, toes, and neck. Then I picked him up and carried him into the house; we were playing again within minutes.

After my son's life was spared, my perspective shifted. If I found myself worried about losing my company, my job, my pride, my lifestyle, or my image, that frightening event popped into my head. I wrote down on a piece of paper, "Michael is alive and well, and nothing else matters."

This reminder helped keep my financial problems in proper perspective. In fact, it still helps me keep my whole life in proper perspective. Every time I start to stress about money or other things, I remember that things could be a lot worse. I choose to thank God for my blessings. Gratitude even became the foundation for writing "God's Promises."

> Things could be a lot worse.

I met with my pastor, and he gave me great verses that I began to meditate on. In my prayer time, I kept finding truths that strongly ministered to my soul. I typed them out and put them on a piece of paper in my wallet. When I started thinking negatively, I would pull out what I called "God's Promises" to get me back on track. I tried to remind myself that in overcoming past crises or tribulations, I always came out a better person afterward.

I've listed below some of my favorite truths. Please remember that this is my personal list. You may be dealing with different challenges than I was or am, but you can still find much to be thankful for.

- Success is not defined by what you have but who you are.
- My success is my walk with God, my marriage, my family, and my friends.
- God has a plan for my life; my destiny is in His hands.
- The trials I go through only make me a better person.
- Pray and listen to God about decisions.
- God has intervened on my behalf several times—in spite of my reluctance to listen to Him. I'm hopeful He will continue to do so.
- Enjoy the ride; you only have one chance at today.
- It doesn't take character in the good times!
- Fight to win! Don't have regrets; you took big chances to make it big.
- I believe in my destiny; I believe I'm supposed to be successful and help many people!

- Don't feel sorry for yourself; behave in a way that would make God proud!

1 Chronicles 4:10 NIV says,

> Jabez cried out to the God of Israel, "Oh, that you would bless me and enlarge my territory! Let your hand be with me, and keep me from harm so that I will be free from pain." And God granted his request.

- Enjoy every minute. So many people have big problems such as death, lack of food, broken relationships, unemployment, and so forth.
- It's all His! It's in His hands, so do the best you can and forget about it!

James 1: 2–4 NIV says,

> Consider it pure joy, my brothers and sisters whenever you face trials of many kinds, because you know that the testing of your faith produces perseverance. Let perseverance finish its work so that you may be mature and complete, not lacking anything.

It's important to meditate on what is right instead of what is wrong. But I must also consider how my circumstances can strengthen me if I allow them to. I can see God if I look for Him, and that seeking has dramatically shaped my life and how I navigate through storms. I would like to challenge you to think about what is right in your life. What would you miss if it were taken away? Try writing a list of what you have to be thankful for. Are there any promises you cling to? Has God promised you anything specifically? Are there any Scriptures that bring you hope, joy, peace, or love? Write them down. Have them ready for when the next storm hits. Then, you can remember who you are in all circumstances and who God always is. He never changes. He is faithful. He will never leave you nor forsake you. You can trust Him to keep His promises!

Chapter 20

Materialism

Motives for Finances

In my journey so far, I have learned that sometimes I had to chase my dreams to find out how empty the material things in life are. I wanted the big house and got it. I wanted the new cars and got them. The glitter quickly wears off, and I was stuck with the costs and reminders of those questionable decisions. Some are better than others, but I quickly realized that *things* are not important in life.

Many people fill their lives with all sorts of things they think will bring them happiness. The most common ones I have seen are pets, food, work, status, money, alcohol, possessions, and leisure activities. They spin their wheels and waste their energies trying to fill a void in their hearts. But eventually, they have to ask themselves the question, what is important?

As I asked myself this question, I realized that true happiness is centered in God. He is the one steady and consistent theme in life. Living for Him is not a guarantee of happiness in every single moment, but it is the only foundation that can provide long-term happiness. When I live for Him, I live into a purpose that is greater than I. I gain a reward that will never need to be maintained or repaired the way possessions do. Don't get me wrong—I enjoy nice things. But it's important to keep them in the proper context.

I recently read about lottery winners who went broke shortly after their windfall and about professional athletes and famous musicians who end up penniless. We can learn from their examples. More money does not equal success or happiness; it is just more money. As we have discussed before, we live in a world where people watch television and see characters that appear to have it all. They enjoy big homes, expensive cars, designer clothes, extravagant travel, and fine jewelry. They seem to be happy. And the underlining message is that their things have brought them happiness. A lot of people think that should be reality but it isn't. It's fantasy. No matter how much money people make, if they lack wisdom about how to handle it, they spend it faster than it comes in.

I have read a lot of financial books written from a Christian perspective, and most have a fairly consistent message. My personal belief is that you should at least set aside 10 percent of your income for giving back and at least another 10 percent as savings. Ideally, you should have six months' income in reserve so that when you have a problematic health or job issue, you do not simultaneously have a financial crisis. Once you deduct your normal living expenses, the remaining money can go toward luxuries. A luxury is anything that is not a necessity—i.e., the newest phone, internet, cable television, eating out, or travel.

And we can always sacrifice our luxuries in order to contribute to other important opportunities including savings, investments, or ministries.

I still remember the moment I began considering who I could help with my available money. I was watching "Schindler's List" for the first time. I sobbed when the main character said he could have sold his ring and saved one more person. It affected me so deeply because I realized that my financial decisions affected lives far beyond my own.

I'm not trying to put a guilt trip on anyone. Let me reiterate that Robyn and I like nice things. But I have learned that seeking God on major purchases and weighing the costs leads to wise financial decisions.

Your enjoyment of life is important. Helping others is important. And none of that comes from being financially irresponsible. Financial stress is one of the top contributors to the dissolution of relationships. So before you spend money on whatever you think will make you happy, be aware of what it might ultimately cost you.

You also need to determine your motivation behind purchases. Are you making any financial decisions to impress others? For example, I see a lot of older couples with huge homes for just the two of them; most of the space sits empty. I wonder about maintaining, heating, and cooling a huge house that is mostly unused. Is that wise?

Sometimes we are trying to prove our success to anyone watching us or even to ourselves. Sometimes we feel that once we have _____, then we will be happy. Sometimes we simply and genuinely enjoy what we've purchased. I promise, however, that you will get more joy out of helping someone than most material items could ever bring you—even momentarily.

What do you need? What are you trying to buy? Instead of selling yourself short by settling for some experience that mimics what you really need, choose to love yourself enough to get what you need to be genuinely happy. Invest in others or a purpose, and truly experience happiness. Once you are in that position, you can enjoy your purchases for what they are. You won't be disappointed by what they didn't supply. Things simply do not bring happiness, and more money doesn't equal success.

Serving and cultivating true relationships with God and others is the key to happiness. Resolve today to make decisions from a place of how you can love God, yourself, and others by serving a bigger purpose with what you have been given. If you do, you will be on the road to lasting, authentic, and true joy—joy that will not need to be maintained and will never wear out. You are worth it.

> You will get more joy out of helping someone.

Chapter 21

Wisdom

Relief of Asking for Help

I am constantly amazed by the gift of asking for wisdom. God first inspired me to do this because perhaps He knew I was a little dense in some areas. Without His wisdom, I would surely have fallen down when I didn't need to.

It was just before my father was diagnosed with liver cancer that I felt the need to pray for wisdom. His diagnosis and subsequent death caused shock and sorrow for those who knew him. Looking back, I understand better why the Holy Spirit inspired me to pray for wisdom. I was able to deal with that devastating event far better than I could have imagined. I had the opportunity to share about Jesus to everyone around me. How amazing that something so painful, handled with wisdom, worked together for good.

Shortly after losing my dad, I read through the entire Bible. When I came to the book of Proverbs, it was like nothing I had ever experienced. I became excited to read every verse, as each conveyed the value of wisdom and understanding. I discovered that the Bible is filled with wisdom about how to navigate through life with love, dignity, and purpose.

If you pray for wisdom and read the Bible to gain understanding, you'll see how wisdom can encompass many prayers. It can answer the following questions.

- How can I get along with my spouse?
- Should I take this new job?
- Is this a fair price?
- Should I marry this person?
- Am I supposed to open this business?
- Should I move to this state?

I'm not recommending that you shouldn't pray about or for specific things. I'm suggesting that by asking the Lord to give you a spirit of wisdom, your prayers might be simplified. If you have plenty of God-given wisdom, you will be able to answer certain questions without much difficulty. God will confirm the answer instead of giving it to you, which is a mark of maturing in the Lord.

Jesus recommends in Matthew 6:7–8 that we keep our prayers short and to the point. He says that He already knows what is troubling us, so we don't need to pray long-winded prayers unless we are trying to impress others. Living in such a way as to impress others rather than God is something that even a small amount of wisdom can remedy.

When you pray for wisdom, you are asking God to divinely impart supernatural intellect into your mind. The result can help you achieve things that are greater than you can ask, think, or imagine! I truly believe that only God has taken me from a person of average intelligence to someone who has authority to speak to and instruct others from experience. God has transformed me from a person who made stupid decisions and mistakes on a regular basis to someone who has formed corporations, sits on boards and committees, and is asked to advise on all kinds of subjects.

I went from a negative net worth to a substantial net worth. I truly believe this transformation is because of my persistent prayer that God impart wisdom and understanding to me. If I've learned anything, it is that I will continue to pray for more wisdom as long as I live. I still have a lot to learn.

A powerful tool for gaining wisdom is to read a chapter from the book of Proverbs each day. There are thirty-one chapters in Proverbs. A very practical way to enjoy this Scripture is to read the chapter that coordinates with the day of the month. So if it is January fourth, you could read Proverbs chapter 4. It doesn't matter how many times I have read over these chapters; I always get more out of them the next time through. It is a disciplined choice that I have never regretted.

Matthew 6:7–8 NIV says,

> And when you pray, do not keep on babbling like pagans, for they think they will be heard because of their many words. Do not be like them, for your Father knows what you need before you ask him.

James 1:5 NIV says,

> If any of you lacks wisdom, you should ask God,
> who gives generously to all without finding fault,
> and it will be given to you.

Chapter 22

Others' Perceptions

Self-Awareness in Relationships

I am continuously fascinated by the topic of how we are perceived. I believe there is some truth to the idea that individual perception determines reality. Therefore, it is really important to understand how other people are reacting to us—to our personalities, our characters, our beliefs, our senses of humor, and our culture. This does not mean we should shift who we are according to our environment, but that we should honor others by acting in ways that would avoid causing hurt or anger.

> Avoid causing hurt or anger.

It never ceases to amaze me when I see people exhibit behavior that makes them appear oblivious to how others perceive them. If it were only arrogance, it would be understandable; arrogant people do not always care how others see them. They believe they are operating on a higher plain. What I am referring to are people who want to be known, liked, and loved.

You can probably say that you have met people you didn't like. Can you define the things you didn't like about them? Were they self-centered? Perhaps they were self-declared authorities on everything, or just downright depressing all the time. Are their lives so terrible that you have to hear about every tragedy, blow by blow?

Well, maybe for someone else that person is you. And maybe someone who could have become a mutually beneficial friend to you decided not to be around you. Can you imagine that you may have not gotten your dream job because someone didn't like the way you carried yourself? Worse yet, what if they were right?

I'm not suggesting that we turn our social lives into an elaborate act to please others. But I do believe it's very healthy to consistently evaluate how others perceive us. I have found a couple ways to do this without losing the essence of who I am.

Here are some questions to ask yourself periodically:

1. How do others react to you?
2. Are they positive?
    a. Do people seem interested in what you have to say?
    b. Do people ask advice or your opinion on things important to them?
    c. Do people confide in you?
    d. Do people trust you?
    e. Do people appear to care about you?

3. Are they negative?
    a. Do people seem distracted when you are with them?
    b. Do people have something important to deal with and need to get away quickly every time you are with them?
    c. Do people seem to avoid getting together with you?
    d. Do you dominate most conversations?
    e. Do you find yourself talking negatively about others?

Make an effort not to talk about yourself all the time. People want you to be interested in them. They want to talk about their interests, their families, and their careers. Guess what? They are more interesting than you are! You know almost everything about yourself, but you probably don't know nearly as much about them. They can teach you new things. And these new things may be interesting to others. Once you choose to listen, you will learn new things to share with others. This trait makes you someone people want to talk to.

Do you like to share your problems with others? Does it make you feel better to vent? Be careful; this type of sharing should only be done with a close friend whom you trust. If it is a healthy relationship, the person will care about your problems and will encourage you. If the person does not, remember that he or she may not be the problem. A person that is always looking for a shoulder to cry on is not the type of person most people enjoy having a relationship with.

If you find that you can't stop complaining, seek an opportunity to obtain some professional guidance to help you work through your circumstances. I would highly recommend seeking pastoral guidance; many churches are prepared to send you in the direction of a recommended counselor or other resources. Healing is a wonderful journey and nothing you need to fear.

Do you find people stubborn? Do they not understand your thoughts or advice on a subject? If you are continuously—and maybe forcefully—sharing with someone who does not want to hear what you're saying, you could be causing more harm than good. Often, people are unaware of how frustrating they can be when they're trying to cram something down another person's throat. I personally find myself so frustrated that I often end up doing the very opposite of their unsolicited recommendations. Strong-arming others with your opinions and advice is one of the most effective ways to clear your social calendar.

"People with personality faults really frustrate me. In fact, did you hear about John? He brought his kids to school with no lunch! Then his wife, Jane! Can you believe her? She lets her daughter dress like a tramp!"

Have you ever heard comments like these? Or have you ever taken part in such a conversation? Most of us have. One of the ways we try to lift ourselves up is by putting others down. This is unhealthy, and nothing could be further from the heart of God. The best way to handle this type of behavior is to speak only positively about others. If someone says that a certain person is bad, you have the opportunity to point out what is right and good.

But this approach still has plenty of tension. It's easy to get sucked in. One way to avoid this pit is to share, simply and honestly, that you no longer wish to speak negatively about people because you are making some life changes. You can be the instrument of the change you wish to see in the world!

In conclusion, people matter. Loving people well matters. If you choose to be slow to speak and quick to listen, you can't go wrong. If you choose to put the needs of others before your own and speak words that lift up instead of tear down, your friends will know they can trust you. If you only share your hurts, drama, and struggles with a few close friends in your life, you will be a blessing to many. You can be a person who is intentionally well received. You can be real without sharing everything. You can be genuinely concerned without always bringing the subject back to yourself. You can! I believe in you.

Chapter 23

Living Healthy for You
Enjoy Taking Care of Yourself

When I was young, I suffered from a really bad back. In a snap, it would just go out. And then I'd look like an elderly man—crippled by arthritis and age—walking around hunched over and moving ever so slowly. I would miss out on some fun activities because I was physically unable to join in. And I wondered if I would battle this condition the rest of my life.

In my late teens, I began rollerblading. I loved it. I could skate so fast that I felt like I was flying. I used to skate for hours, enjoying the feel of the speed and wind. And through all this rollerblading, my core became stronger. The stronger my core became the less often my back went out. Sometimes rollerblading felt like work. However, I knew I would enjoy the experience once I was out on my blades. I also knew that if I didn't go, I would risk my back going out. This realization added plenty of motivation.

Being healthy is a gift. Many people would give anything to experience a fully functioning, able body. Yet, many of us don't appreciate our carefully crafted bodies that run like well-oiled machines. But machines need maintenance to work well, and our bodies are the same. Certain types of foods and fluids are necessary for our bodies to properly function. If we have bodies that are working for us, do we not have a certain amount of responsibility to maintain them well?

There is so much fitness hype. On social media we see hashtags about being fit; many people on our newsfeeds are becoming focused and determined athletes. We see extremism in every arena of life including fitness. This approach can leave us feeling ashamed and stuck in an unhealthy rut. I want to suggest a different message altogether. What if we approach fitness in terms of making consistent choices, motivated by loving ourselves and our lives?

How you feel about *you* matters. What choice are you making today to show yourself that? How you feel physically matters. Are there any physical issues holding you back? What choice are you making today to change that reality?

I love tennis, so that's how I exercise. After one session with my best friend, he said, "You know, you could be huge if you lifted weights!" I replied, "I don't want to be huge." You see, working out is not my passion. But I do want to be healthy. Therefore, I exercise by doing something that's fun for me. I also choose to eat and drink what helps me feel energized and alive. I aim to get enough sleep so that I don't start my day already feeling depleted. And I have found that if I am consistent, I do not have to kill myself to achieve my desired results. It really doesn't take much effort, so give it as much as you have.

There are simple ways to introduce activity into your life. You can take the stairs instead of the elevator. You can choose to park in the back of the parking lot instead of looking for the closest spot. If you look for the less convenient way of doing something that takes more exertion, you will find it. The hard part will be actually choosing it! Once you begin, however, you will become hungry for more healthy routines.

It is scientifically proven that exercise releases the happy hormones in the brain. So exercising is a natural way to feel happy, relaxed, and stress-free. When my life was crumbling financially, playing tennis was my prescription for joy. I would go out on the court—all knotted up with worry and stress—and I would leave feeling happy, light, and thankful for life and friends. I also felt more motivated and less focused on negative thoughts.

They say it only takes twenty-one days to create a habit. So, begin by making one small change, and then do it consistently for three weeks. Once you have made that your new normal, add another small change. In no time at all, you can create the healthy lifestyle you have longed to enjoy. Trying to change everything all at once works for some, but it leaves many feeling hopeless about actually enjoying the change they desire.

Motive also matters. If you are virtually living at the gym, ask yourself why. If it's your passion and you love it, then keep it up! But if you dread the gym, maybe there is another activity you would enjoy more. If you aren't exercising at all, ask yourself why you don't love *you* enough to take care of the body you have been given? This sort of self-examination may be difficult, but you are worth being a priority to yourself!

If you are eating only super-healthy, protein-packed (but possibly flavor-lacking) food all the time, ask yourself who you are eating for? Again, if this is for you, that is great! But if you resent eating healthy all the time and are tempted to binge on sweets, find some balance. You can make the majority of your choices healthy, and allow yourself to eat a few items you love that aren't necessarily good for you.

I recently heard that it is easier to exercise thirty minutes of self-control in the grocery store than to exercise it twenty-four hours a day at home. Making choices to support your goals is a great start! There is nothing wrong with being super fit and healthy, but there is something off about being so strict that you miss out altogether on some of life's pleasures. Find the balance and enjoy the journey!

Chapter 24

Be Ready for Anything

Intentional Mental Preparation

There is wisdom in not worrying about the future. Worry indicates fear and anxiety. It can leave you feeling out of control, weary, nervous, and even hopeless. I have often avoided worry through a mental exercise I began practicing long ago: I walk through the *what-ifs* that attempt to plague my life. I go through the ugly ones—my biggest fears. I consider what would happen if this or that occurred and work through the possible consequences. I have found one thing to be true: I am an overcomer. It is my nature. I find a way to overcome through prayer, faith, learning from circumstances, and adapting to my new normal. I determine to use for good every struggle in my life and in the lives of others.

We can find freedom if we determine to be constantly ready for the unexpected. We should mentally prepare ourselves for dealing with painful things; they happen to people every single day. One day it could be me, or it could be you. Adverse circumstances, tragedy, disease, financial disaster—these are real things that happen. We should be prepared for them. We need to have a plan or strategy in place about how to overcome hardships before they strike.

If you have an enemy who totally wants to defeat you, let's think about the most strategic plan of attack to defeat that enemy. In a military battle, the strategy is to strike enemies at their weakest points in order to break through their battle lines. Consider a lion that's watching a herd of animals he wants to prey on. The lion looks for the young, wounded, or the weak to attack. It is not as much work and is highly effective. Your enemy is not above kicking you while you are down. Therefore, if tragedy hits in your life and you are unprepared, you are more vulnerable to attack. But it doesn't have to be that way.

Let's consider what you need to mentally prepare for. Are you ready for anything? Can you handle losing your job? Have you thought about how you would react if you lost your spouse, parent, or child? What about being diagnosed with a disease that will take your life or dramatically alter it? Or what about the smaller, unexpected hardships like getting sick or hurt, your car breaking down, or a fire destroying your possessions? If you haven't considered how such events could affect your life, it would be wise to think through some of these scenarios. The purpose is not to worry or be fearful but to relieve those anxieties.

Consider who you are and what you are made of. Consider who God is and what He offers you. When you are faced with tragedy, you have a unique opportunity to react in a way that glorifies God. Most people question God when tragedy hits no matter how long they have been walking with Him or how well they know Him.

Why is it that we question the One we can trust when we need Him the most? Do you think this is a coincidence? I think not. I believe the Enemy has encouraged doubt in order to keep us disconnected from hope in times of trouble. Instead, we can resolve in advance to know, believe, and act on what is true even when it's painful, dark, or just plain hard. We can access the source that will truly fill us with all we need. Through this connection, we will be equipped to deal with loss and eventually use our pain to bless and help others.

God uses the trials of life to develop traits such as perseverance, endurance, patience, belief, hope, love, integrity, and compassion. When I fail to respond in a manner that is pleasing to God—by hardening my heart, becoming bitter, choosing unforgivness, or remaining just plain mad—then I am setting myself up to face the same or a similar trail again.

Now, I'm not suggesting that you or I shouldn't go through the grieving process if someone we love dies. We have to have reasonable expectations for ourselves. I'm simply saying that when we experience fear around a tragic event, we should stop and see how God might use and work His will through it.

For example, losing your job might seem like a tragedy; your new circumstances, however, may expose an opportunity you never would have seen otherwise. So if you still have your job but fear losing it, take time to walk through what you can do to bounce back and how you can face potential hardship with thanksgiving and peace. You have to trust that if you belong to God, He will be true to His Word and use everything in your life for a good purpose.

I personally experienced the benefit of this mental resolve during the period of time when my parents passed away. My dad got the news of his illness and died a short time later. Less than two years afterward, my mom also passed away. I had spent time mentally preparing for the loss of my parents, although I never imagined it would be so soon or so close together. But because I had already considered the loss, a certain amount of surprise was not a part of my emotional grieving. I still miss my parents to this day. But because I was somewhat prepared for their loss, I enjoyed the memories of their lives much sooner than I had ever considered possible.

> Determine to be ready for the unexpected.

We have to be adaptable. The world is changing faster than ever. The internet and other technologies are creating new careers and eliminating others. People who are willing to adapt to change are typically the ones who end up being blessed, not hindered, by transitions. Change is part of life. You don't have to be afraid, but you can be prepared.

Do you need to take some additional steps to work through some of your fears? I challenge you to ask yourself the following questions. Pray through them with God. Work through your fears one at a time for as long as it takes. You will find freedom and peace as a result!

1. What is my biggest fear?
2. What would happen to me if it actually happened?
3. What good could come as a result of it happening?
4. What could I learn about myself as I face this possibility?
5. Who could I help if I had to go through it?
6. How could I avoid questioning the goodness of God if it happened to me?
7. What can I do now to keep from spinning out of control as a result of unexpected events or tragedies?

Chapter 25

Judging Others
Drawing Well-informed Conclusions

Our society loves to put people down. We make comparisons and then try to make ourselves appear better than others. I assume it is a way—a very poor way—to deal with our own insecurities. This became apparent to me when I watched the movie "The General's Daughter." In the movie, the daughter is a gorgeous, intelligent young lady. Not only is she promiscuous, but she ventures into deviant sexual behavior.

I thought as I watched, *What a terrible character. She could be such a great person, but instead she's throwing her life away.* But then the movie took a turn by revealing past events that led to the current situation. The main character had been out on a military exercise when she became the victim of a gang rape. Her father responded by sweeping the event under the rug for political reasons instead of fighting for his daughter. As a result, she didn't know how to deal with this horrific event. Her inability to heal or even give voice to what had happened caused her to spiral into the bizarre behaviors I judged her for.

I saw only a small portion of the whole story and made an assumption about who she was, who she could be, and what she should be doing differently. I did not take the time to understand why she acted the way she did. I did not consider a broader perspective of the situation. I simply decided that I knew what was better for her than she did.

Even though I'm referring to a movie, real life offers similar scenarios. We don't know people's pasts, wounds, trials, or how far they have come. We have no grounds to judge them for where they are in life. For example, some Christians like to carry picket signs and go after the gay community. How do you think Jesus would handle that situation? I think He would love everyone and draw them into His kingdom with compassion and kindness. Our job is not to be the Christian police; it is to draw them to God by loving, caring, listening, and sharing our faith, hope, and strength with others.

Once people enter into a close relationship with God, He can convict their hearts about where freedom or breakthroughs are needed. If we are going to rally around particular sins, what do you think about picketing all the fast food restaurants or buffets, shaming patrons for giving in to gluttony? Would that change the outcome at all? Would that really impact those patrons? That type of behavior—judgment—will never accomplish the desired result.

If you really love others and see areas where freedom is needed, your most loving act is to pray for them. Ask the Lord to reveal to them what's needed and to give them a teachable spirit. He doesn't need you to act as the Holy Spirit in their lives. Take time to love others and know them. Be a voice that celebrates progress in their lives and shares their vulnerabilities and struggles. By being real and open with others, you may find yourself in a position to point them toward God's purpose.

There is a big difference between judgment and accountability. You have to earn the right to hold someone accountable. You must be privy to their convictions and have more than a sliver of information about who they are, why they are the way they are, and who they want to become. I do not believe you are able to hold strangers accountable.

> Be a voice that celebrates progress.

If you find yourself wanting to bring correction into a stranger's life without knowing them through relationship, check your motives. There is a good chance you would be speaking, praying, or acting out of judgment.

Jesus said,

> Do not judge, or you too will be judged. For in the same way you judge others, you will be judged, and with the measure you use, it will be measured to you. Why do you look at the speck of sawdust in your brother's eye and pay no attention to the plank in your own eye? How can you say to your brother, 'Let me take the speck out of your eye,' when all the time there is a plank in your own eye? You hypocrite, first take the plank out of your own eye, and then you will see clearly

to remove the speck from your brother's eye.
(Matthew 7:1–5 NIV)

These verses show that most of us are more prone to look at someone else's imperfections while ignoring the areas in our own lives that need improvement. What if we chose to actively seek the Lord about issues in our lives? What if we vulnerably shared about how He is teaching and refining us? What if we allowed the organic overflow of that to impact the lives of others?

Let's only give advice when we are asked; even then, take that opportunity to teach others how to ask God for themselves. We can be a greater example by simply living for Christ and letting people observe us than we can by ignoring our own the flaws and using our words to correct others.

So who do you regularly judge without knowing the whole of their story? Who do you feel better than? What struggles do people face that make you want to shake them, give them the solution, and make them better? Well, how is that working for you or for them? Instead of wasting time and energy focusing on things we have no control over, let's focus on what we do have control over: ourselves. Here are some questions to ponder.

1. What could be the proverbial log in your eye right now?
2. What would it take to remove it?
3. What steps can you take toward that?
4. Is there anyone you need to apologize to regarding your harsh judgment about his or her life?

5. Is there any particular struggle in the lives of others that could benefit from a perspective change?

Learning not to judge others is a process. Most of us have lived lives full of judgment, so it may take a while to notice when we are judging. Just try to remember that we probably do not know the whole story. And if we have never walked in another person's shoes, we really can't say what we would do in his or her place. We need to focus on our own stuff and be real about our individual processes with those in our inner circles. We need to allow the fruit of vulnerability to affect others in a benevolent way. We can do it!

Chapter 26

Living Example

Being Vulnerable on Purpose

When I was young, I had two older brothers who really lived for Jesus. Their examples greatly affected my life. I was invited to a Young Life camp and dedicated my life to Jesus at an early age. But after that, I struggled with actually living according to the Word of God. I met a pastor in Daytona Beach who loved me through all my rebellious behaviors. I never even smelled a hint of judgment—just love. It was extravagant love with no condemnation and was the reflection of Christ on earth. That is what won my heart. And because I experienced this love as a young person, I want to extend it to others.

I have failed in major ways to live according to the Word of God. And yet, I have also majorly succeeded. Despite my imperfections, my hope is that my lifestyle reflects love. My goal is that others will experience God's loving perception of them through their interactions with me. I intentionally treat each person with love and honor. I have found that it is the number-one way to win others to the Lord.

This applies to parenting too. My wife and I made it our goal to show Christ to our kids through vulnerability and honesty. We wanted our lives in the world to be consistent with our home lives. We didn't want to promote any illusions about ourselves. Our prayers and hopes were that our home would be a place of invitation and welcome to others. Our kids' friends, one after another, have told us how much they appreciated and benefited from the atmosphere of our home. The peace and joy they experienced while staying with us was refreshing. We created that atmosphere by taking the time to truly see and get to know our children's friends as individuals.

If you want to share the gospel but you do not really care about an individual, what is your motive exactly?

One really important factor in living a life of love is to remember that God saves and rescues. Knowing that God is the giver of this faith-based life (not you) protects you from thinking you are all that! Without humility, people will not feel safe enough to be real or vulnerable with you. They might think you do not face challenges like they do. But by handling your challenges with humility and vulnerability, you can share how God has partnered with you to help you overcome them. This sharing will be the catalyst that causes anyone who needs Jesus to come running. Your life's journey is about how you are equipped to share His love with others in the midst of their struggles. It is one reason we can rejoice in our trials.

Here are some questions to ask yourself and/or God to see how you are living as an example of God's love to others.

1. Are my words and ideas about living a life of love consistent with my actions?
2. Am I treating the people I interact with daily with love and honor?
3. Am I sharing my journey vulnerably where God is asking me to, or am I pretending I have it all together?
4. Am I hurting others with my judgments about them?

We all have work to do in living out divine love. Choose to celebrate where you have made progress. Get excited about where you can make small shifts to change someone's life forever—most likely, your own!

Chapter 27

Prayer

Talking with God

Prayer has been a huge gift in my life, though I do not consider myself really great at it. Simply put, prayer is nothing more than having a conversation with God; it is conversation consisting of both talking and listening. It is neither formal nor forced, and it has become part of my routine. Although I have set aside special quiet times of concentrated prayer, I am praying all day long. God is with me constantly, and the best way for me to understand and live from that reality is by speaking to Him about everything. I've learned that nothing is too small or too big to pray about, and there is never a wrong time to pray.

To elaborate on what I shared earlier in the marriage nugget, I'm often asked how I pray. In trying to answer, I would like to share what I have learned so far.

A long time ago, I was introduced to a very practical way to pray through a ministry known as Navigators. Since then, I pray using the acronym ACTS or adoration, confession, thanksgiving, and supplication. I usually begin with the Lord's Prayer (Matthew

6:9–13) and then go through the acronym. I show God *adoration.* Sometimes I sing—which is not pretty—and sometimes I don't. I often talk about how big and wonderful He is and how constant and trustworthy He has proven Himself throughout every facet of life. For *confession*, I simply confess my sins before God. I repent of the sins I see, the sins I am unaware of, and the sins of omission—when I should have done something but didn't. I ask for and receive His forgiveness. Next is *thanksgiving.* I just thank Him for everything I can think of: my health, the people in my life, His grace, His love, and so forth. The last step is *supplication.* This is where I ask for help with areas of life that are troubling me. But usually, these problems appear less significant through the course of my prayer. I also use this time to pray for other people: family members, friends, and our team at the office.

Another question I'm frequently asked is when do I pray or what is the right or best time to pray? My answer is that I tend to have more concentrated prayer time in the evenings, although most people I know have their best success praying in the morning. I also try to use any down time as an opportunity to pray: toilet time, drive time, night time when I'm awake, or waiting situations anywhere. I also pray throughout the day.

I have friends who are far more *prayer aware* than I am. They ask God about what shirt to wear, which route to drive to work, what to eat, or when to speak. Although I still have room to grow, I have never regretted time spent in prayer. I am so thankful that I can ask God for wisdom, revelation, hope, joy, peace, and love for others and myself. There are few things more exciting than witnessing answered prayers.

Have you ever wondered *why* people pray? Prayer keeps me from forgetting how much I need God. It keeps my ego from getting out of hand. As I have sought Him in prayer, asking for wisdom and guidance, He has helped me miss landmines that I otherwise would have stepped on. A friend of mine, who is not a believer, could not understand why God would want us to shower Him with adoration. My friend asked, "Is God insecure or arrogant?"

> Prayer keeps me from forgetting how much I need God.

My theory is that He knows we have a tendency to think that the world rotates around us. By putting our focus on Him and humbling ourselves before Him, we are in a much healthier frame of mind. The best way to sum it up is that He doesn't need us, but we need Him.

Prayer also helps us to see others instead of just thinking about ourselves. A former pastor of mine used to say that if you are struggling in any area, pray for someone else who is also struggling in that area. This suggestion has proved to be far more productive than just thinking about my own struggle or thinking that I am alone in my struggle. The best and most powerful place to pray is from the place of experience. So in the moments when you are in the fray and acquainted with the pain of particular circumstances, you can be extremely effective. Pray for those going through the same thing at the same time.

And lastly, remember how powerful it is to pray for your *enemies.* When I get mad at someone, I pray for him or her. When someone cuts me off in traffic, I pray for that person. When someone abuses authority and it negatively affects me or someone I care about, I pray for that person. I pray for my friends, and I pray for my enemies. It's becoming a joyous habit. It's shutting the Devil out and blessing others. What a great use of my emotion, time, and energy!

Here are some questions to consider with regard to your prayer life.

1. Is your prayer life how you want it?
2. How could you start inviting God into your daily (mundane) moments?
3. Do you have an enemy you could be praying for?
4. Is anyone you know going through a similar circumstance who could be added to your prayer time?

Chapter 28

Hearing God's Voice
God Talking with You

One of the most beneficial lessons I ever learned is that I can hear God's voice. We took classes at a church that were simply called "Hearing God's Voice." We learned several ways that God communicates with us. The most important thing to do is try to hear Him. In Jeremiah 29:13 NIV we learn,

> You will seek me and find me when you seek me
> with all your heart.

When God speaks, it is not often in a thundering or booming voice. Instead, He tends to speak with a still small voice. This means that I must be still to hear Him. The noise of this world can easily drown out God's voice, so I have to make an intentional effort to hear His leading, wisdom, love, and guidance. And the more I attune my hearing and make myself available to listen to Him, the clearer His voice becomes.

God is also very creative when it comes to speaking to His children. Oftentimes, He will speak to them in their own language.

For example, I know a lot of people who work in the medical field. And they see pictures and metaphors drawn from a medical perspective that wouldn't mean anything to me. And then there are my friends who love to cook. They gain understanding from the processes and overlapping principles of cooking.

God will most likely speak to you through things you are familiar with. He speaks to each of us differently. Some people receive words, and some receive pictures. Some see visions, and some have dreams. We cannot limit God. And we need to decide it is okay if we do not understand all His ways. It is exciting when God speaks, but we must also recognize that He speaks with a purpose. When God shares something with us, it is because He loves us and knows that we need more of His guidance.

> What He speaks has also already been written.

When I first started hearing from God, I needed to know how I could be absolutely sure it was God's voice. One of the first principles I learned was that God never speaks something that is not confirmed in His Word. He never changes. What He speaks has also already been written. Always check to see that what you are hearing in your spirit is in accordance with the Bible. You can even ask the Lord to show you that what He just spoke to your heart is in His Word. He has never denied me this request.

I have heard it shared that the Lord is always speaking, but we might not always be listening. As with radio frequencies, they are broadcasting all the time, but the only time we can hear them is when we tune in. I believe this idea can be applied to God's communication. Every time I have asked the Lord to attune my ears to His voice—and I take the time to still my heart and mind to listen—His voice is clear. This world has plenty of hustle and bustle, which makes it difficult to be still. At times, it can even feel awkward to be with myself and ignore distractions. But I have never regretted spending time with God. It takes discipline, but the reward is greater than the cost.

I have gone through seasons when it seemed that God had stopped speaking. This happened during my financial crisis, which was also an emotionally low season of my life. I felt as though I could not hear Him speak. But I have since gained some perspective on that experience. Consider a surgeon in the operating room. The surgeon doesn't speak to the patient in the middle of the operation. It is a delicate time, and the procedure must be handled with great care.

And so it is with seasons of deep, almost surgical pain. In each moment of such days I must choose to believe what I have based my whole life on: God is always good, and I am always loved. He has a plan for my life and is always acting in my best interest. I can trust Him. He doesn't change. If I can't hear Him, I don't have to question Him. And that is the key to getting through the silence: do not question what you know to be true when you need it the most. Usually, at the end of a quiet season, I hear more than I ever have heard before.

It is so important that you do not believe the lie that God speaks to others but not to you. You are not dependent on others to hear and relate what God is saying to you. One time, I was about to short sale some properties I was upside down on, and I didn't have total peace that I was making a wise choice. Robyn and I prayed, and I heard God say, "Hold steadfast." Robyn also heard that we were not supposed to move in that direction. We immediately obeyed and changed plans. It was a harder road at first, but obedience always led us into His will. And that choice has been worth it many times over. If I had been waiting on someone else to get my answer from God for me, I might have missed that moment. But I am His child, and I know His voice. He will also speak to you and answer your questions.

Learning to hear His voice doesn't happen on day one. We are always learning. If we want to hear His voice, here are some practical steps we can take.

1. Set aside time each day to quiet your spirit and eliminate distractions. It's preferable to create a peaceful atmosphere.
2. Read from the Bible, and ask God a question about something you have read that you do not understand.
3. Write down in a journal what you hear.
4. Press for more information. Ask more questions.
5. One of my favorite questions to ask is, "Lord, is there anything it would please you to share with me?"
6. Enjoy Him! Enjoy how He uniquely speaks to you! Enjoy finding His voice in Scripture; enjoy getting to know Him!

Chapter 29

Joy of God's Word
Embracing an Absolute

As a Christian, I have enjoyed the gift of having a manual to live by. I am so thankful to have a written moral compass and to know that absolute principles in the Bible can shape a life of purpose. Jesus is my Lord and Savior, and I am completely devoted to following Him and becoming more like Him. The only successful way I have learned to honor this passion and purpose is by studying and thinking on His Word every day.

> The Bible is comprehensible.

One of the biggest lies out there is that the Bible is incomprehensible. Don't quit before actually beginning. Try shifting perspective. You do not have to rush through the Bible. It is supposed to be a lifelong discipline. Therefore, it's okay if it takes you the rest of your life to work through it. Start small.

One of my favorite ways to begin is by reading through what is known as the Gospels. Through the books of Matthew, Mark, Luke, and John, you can get to know the personality of Jesus.

Jesus came to show us how to live as human beings on the earth, connected to God the Father. He showed us what is right, what is available, and what is possible. He gave us a picture of a life poured out in love. I never tire of reading the accounts of the life of Jesus. No matter how many times I have read through them, I am constantly learning something new, deep, fresh, and relevant.

When you are ready to move beyond the Gospels, I urge you to read a chapter out of the book of Psalms and Proverbs every day. The book of Psalms is such a gift because it is a book in which every emotion of the human soul is evident. You find the highest of highs, the lowest of lows, and every emotion in between. You discover that God doesn't change regardless of our emotions. He is the common thread weaving together all the pieces of our lives into a wonderful masterpiece. As we influence others, more and more wisdom is required. And yet, the same words applied to different circumstances still hold true and bring peace. You might view a proverb as common sense one day. When you apply it to a different situation, however, it may seem like a brand new idea. Searching the Scriptures for wisdom is something you will never regret doing.

I have also found that it's easy to get distracted and lose sight of what is important and true. For me, reading the Word of God helps me stay on track. The truth of the Bible is unquestionable; it therefore holds my thoughts and actions accountable through its teachings. Living according to the Bible has kept me from so much destruction in life.

Even if you do not believe in God, living by the principles in the Bible will fill you with integrity, honor, and joy. If you do believe, one essential component to recognize is that you cannot gain the full revelation of God's Word without asking the Holy Spirit for help. Before I begin reading, I say a simple prayer and ask the Holy Spirit to read with me. I ask that He give me eyes to see and ears to hear the truth. I also ask Him to show me any encouragement He wants me to extend to others.

Some really cool tools are available to help us understand what we are reading, when it was written, and how to apply its message in the context of our current culture. One of my favorite tools is a free email service called "Daily Verse." Also, there are some helpful Bible apps for smart phones, which have multiple and even audio versions. My favorite free app is called "YouVersion." Finding a great book on a particular topic or portion of Scripture is also helpful. Some of the most popular books are: *My Utmost for His Highest,* by Oswald Chambers, *Jesus Calling,* by Sarah Young, and *Streams in the Desert,* by Charles Cowman. Many of the Bible apps have a large assortment of free devotionals and reading plans.

It is advisable that you find a version of the Bible that is comprehensible to you. It's also important that you set a "God appointment" in your calendar by scheduling a time to pray to God and read the Bible with Him. Decide how you will allow what you read to influence your life and the lives of others each day. When you start expressing outwardly what you are taking in, you will see the impact of His presence, His truth, and His Word. How exciting!

Chapter 30

Failing Successfully

Getting Back Up

Failing is the most crucial component to becoming who you were created to be. Almost every book on leadership I've read or speech I've heard attributes the majority of success to the process of failing, learning, and moving forward.

If you aren't failing, you're failing; you are playing it safe. If nothing you are up to is too big, too hard, or out of your comfort zone, then you aren't dreaming, trying, or pushing into anything new. You could be on track to miss the most fulfilling parts of you.

Consider Thomas Edison's famous quotation: "I have not failed. I have just found ten thousand ways that did not work." Where would our world be if he had not persevered? Can you imagine being a person with enough vision to keep trying after ten thousand attempts? Because he kept on believing and trying, our whole world benefited.

You also have something inside of you that others can benefit from. Sometimes it is just the effect of you living a full, wholehearted life. Sometimes the contribution is communicated in a book, a product, or an invention. Whatever it is, it matters, as you and your influence on others matter.

A journey can seem so daunting when you try to climb the whole mountain in a single step. It seems impossible and perhaps not even worth trying. That is how it looked to me when the economy tanked. I was a million dollars in debt to my company, losing upward of thirty thousand dollars per month. I had thirteen properties that I could not afford to pay the mortgages on. I looked at all of the pieces as a whole and concluded I was sunk.

> Failure was more profitable than success.

I sat in that belief for a second before I realized that such thinking would keep me stuck. So I decided that even though I saw a bunch of hurdles I could only take one step at a time. And then another and another. I took one hurdle at a time. Once I conquered one, the next one didn't seem as high. Then after two, I began believing "I can do this—it's not that bad." About halfway through, I looked back and saw how much I had overcome. That became my motivation to continue moving forward.

I had played big, risked big, and lost big—but I was actually winning. You see, the choice to keep going, in spite of the failing, was actually winning. I found out what was important and what wasn't. I discovered deeper truths about life, losing, enduring, spending, saving, community, joy, and hope. Because of the knowledge gained in this way, failure was more profitable than success.

Many others were also negatively affected when the economy crashed. However, most of the successful people bounced back. And it wasn't just that they bounced back; they came back better than before. They now run better businesses. They exercise more wisdom in terms of their spending. They handle all the aspects of their businesses with greater detail and efficiency. And many are now planning and preparing for the bottom to drop out again. If there is a next time, many will not be hit as hard as they were the first time. Failure made them better businessmen and businesswomen—truly a gift learned through hard circumstances.

Let me make an important point here: do not fail to simply fail. It is important to calculate the risk and to be sure the risk is worth the reward. Before you leap, you need to count the cost. In the past, I would have done almost anything to become a billionaire—even if it meant leveraging my successful company to acquire many other companies. That is no longer my desire. I am not willing to risk the farm for greater financial possibility. Could I be missing out on a lot of money? Potentially, yes. But is the associated stress and risk worth it? For me, the answer is no.

This book came from a lifetime of failing, learning, and trying again. I now know it is just as important to learn what doesn't work and what I'm not meant to be. I am okay with either outcome. To define failing, I have to know my own definition of success. Success to me means learning from mistakes, not giving up, and finishing my race well.

Are you just sitting in failure and thinking it will be the end of your story? Are you staying stuck because none of it turned out the way you thought it would?

I am extending my hand to you. It is time to stand up again. This isn't the end for you. Your story is not concluded. You still get to write the page-turner about the one who comes back with unpredictable fierceness. You still have opportunities to become more and enjoy the journey again. You are more equipped than ever if you choose to learn from your past experiences. So stand up and get moving. It's a new day.

Question to ponder about failing.

1. How do you define success for yourself?
2. What lessons have you learned from failing?
3. Is there something you want to do that you are afraid to begin because you could fail?
4. If it fails, what could happen to you? Is the risk worth the possible reward?
5. Who benefits from the outcome being what you hope it will be?
6. What step could you take this week to get started?

About the Author

Guy Bouchard was born in Minnesota and is a self-proclaimed nonconformist who personally faced a near-death experience. He is a husband of twenty-five years and a father to three dynamic children. Guy is the founder and president of multiple companies including Global Resort Homes, one of the largest and best-rated vacation home providers for the Central Florida area. He is a passionate entrepreneur who loves helping businesses succeed and commerce to thrive. He is good at adapting to change and recognizing opportunity.

During his childhood, Guy's family frequently relocated. He learned quickly to find stability and security within people, not things. His parents taught him how to dream and not be afraid to fail. Guy has found much success in life and gives credit mostly to the women who have loved him immensely and believed in him even when, by his own standards, they shouldn't have. His mom and wife, Robyn, have always told him he would be successful; they pushed him to become more when he admittedly would have settled for far less.

Guy has always had a love for God. He is committed to living a life of integrity by trying to make choices pleasing to God and resolves to seek the Lord for wisdom and understanding in all things and at all times. One of the best and hardest things shaping Guy's life is this prayer: "Make me more like You." He is determined to have money without letting money have him. He is dedicated to changing the world by maintaining a humble heart. He is committed to loving family and friends extravagantly and to showing the world God's love. He is willing to serve God, his family, and others in order to make the most difference. Currently, that is the driving force behind releasing *Life's Golden Nuggets*. His heart's desire is to give whatever wisdom he can to following generations so that they can learn from his journey and accelerate their own growth and success.

About the Coauthor

Coauthor Jenna Sartor was born and raised a native Floridian. She has enjoyed twelve years of marriage and currently spends the majority of her time raising her two young sons. Jenna has always been a passionate entrepreneur. She has created and sold multiple businesses. Jenna's current line of business is being a Certified Elite Life Coach. Jenna is passionate about helping people uncover and remember the dreams inside of themselves by encouraging them take the necessary steps to bring those dreams into reality. You can find out more by visiting her website at www.becomingucoaching.com.

When Jenna was fifteen years old she heard God calling her name and she responded by giving her life to Jesus. As a believer, one of the main passions in her heart is that every person, everywhere, would have the opportunity to come into the revelation of how great God's love is for them personally. One way Jenna endeavors to carry out this call is through writing her blog, which you can find at www.layeredhearts.com and also through the writing of this book.

Jenna is a deep contemplative thinker, as well as, really witty. She is a great listener and yet never runs short on encouraging words to share. She laughs with all of her heart, and she loves, really loves, people. Many say of Jenna that she has wisdom beyond her years, which she credits to spending time with God daily. If you could sit across from her, with no doubt she would say to you, while looking into your eyes all the way down to your very soul, "Right now, just the way you are is enough. Serve God by inviting Him to teach you how to love Him, yourself, and others and then truly nothing will be impossible for you."

Recommended Reading List

Here is a list of books that have personally affected our lives. If you are hungry to keep learning and do not know where to begin, this list—though certainly not exhaustive—can provide some helpful options.

- Tony Robbins, *Re-Awaken the Giant Within You*
- Joyce Meyers, *Battlefield of the Mind*
- Brene' Brown, *I Thought It Was Just Me*
- Dr. Henry Cloud and Dr. John Townsend, *Boundaries*
- George Clason, *The Richest Man in Babylon*
- Robert Kiyosaki, *Rich Dad, Poor Dad*
- Dr. Emerson Eggerichs, *Love and Respect*
- Gary Chapman, *The 5 Love Languages*
- Richard Stearns, *The Hole in Our Gospel*
- Sarah Young, *Jesus Calling*
- Bruce Wilkinson, *Prayer of Jabez*
- Ann Voskamp, *One Thousand Gifts*
- Josh McDowell, *Evidence That Demands a Verdict*
- Bill Johnson, *Dreaming with God*

Printed in the United States
By Bookmasters